DREARY
AND IZZY

DREARY AND IZZY

TARA BEAGAN

Playwrights Canada Press
Toronto • Canada

Playwrights Canada Press
The Canadian Drama Publisher
215 Spadina Ave., Suite 230, Toronto, Ontario CANADA M5T 2C7
416.703.0013   fax 416.408.3402
orders@playwrightscanada.com • www.playwrightscanada.com

This book would be twice its cover price were it not for the support of Canadian taxpayers through the Government of Canada Book Publishing Industry Development Programme, Canada Council for the Arts, Ontario Arts Council, and the Ontario Media Development Corporation.

Cover photograph of Tara and Rebecca Beagan by Pauline Beagan.
Cover concept by Patrick Beagan. Cover design: JLArt
Production Editor: MZK

Library and Archives Canada Cataloguing in Publication

Beagan, Tara
    Dreary and Izzy / Tara Beagan.

A play.
ISBN 978-0-88754-612-9

    I. Title.

PS8603.E34D74 2007   C812'.6   C2007-904203-1

First edition: July 2007.
Printed and bound by Canadian Printco Ltd. at Scarborough, Canada.

Love and thanks to my sister bears repeating... Becky, you were my first friend, you are my dearest friend. You taught me how to give and receive love at the same time. So much of my heart is you, and I am a better person because of it. This play is from my heart and so it is as much your creation as it is mine.

• PLAYWRIGHT'S NOTES •

There are many contentious issues within the story that is *Dreary and Izzy* – the neglect of our varying health care systems that led to the denial of Fetal Alcohol Spectrum Disorders for centuries, the infantilization of our First Nations people by the Canadian government, the legacy of dispossession between First Nations and "non" that continues to effect all of Canada's peoples, and the myriad identity questions that spring from adoption. None of these are at the core of this play.

When I first brought *Dreary and Izzy* to Yvette Nolan at Native Earth Performing Arts, she spoke so eloquently about many of these issues, and how most importantly, the play is actually "about the things we'll do for love." I came to realize, through the development of the play and the ensuing production, just how true this is.

The story came to me at the point in time where the play ends. In that strange and wonderful place between sleeping and waking, I dreamt a scene between two sisters. I was moved to write several pages about these sisters and eventually came to know Deirdre and Isabelle as well as I do old friends of mine. People who have seen the play have shared with me stories of their own: the slow and painful loss of a mother to the deterioration of Alzheimer's, the recognition from a teacher of all too many students in the underdeveloped woman-child Isabelle, the embarrassed and vulnerable admissions from a sixteen-year-old who sees in the smitten Deirdre her own high school experiences with love. It is my hope that this play will continue to move people beyond the specifics and speak to some experience they have had, while leaving the residue of these sisters as newer memories.

• ACKNOWLEDGEMENTS •

First and foremost, I thank my sister Becky who introduced me to the term "FAS." Beyond mere science, you take this epidemic very personally and you spoke of it with such passion that I was driven to research FAS. You've always been my favourite teacher.

To the late Michael Dorris whose book, *The Broken Cord*, taught me more than I could ever have gleaned from medical journals.

To Bonnie Buxton, author of the definitive Canadian book on FASD, *Damaged Angels*. Your insight into this subject and all of its related heartbreak brought my understanding of this preventable malady to a very restless place. It drove me through the difficult writing times, knowing how bloody challenging it's been for you. Bonnie, you accepted me into this from the beginning and you continue to inspire with your generosity and courage. Thanks also to your Colette who stood up at that meeting on that fateful day and cursed out the people she saw as being unsupportive of this play – so much like her mother!

Thanks to Ruth Madoc-Jones who let me discover my playwright and for keeping me afloat through the stormy waters.

Gookschem to Cowboy Nolan, reluctant leader and apprehensive mentor – it was through your encouragement that I brought this seed of an idea to the place where it could be staged. Your faith in the collaborative process of theatre is a lesson that I continue to learn. Thank you for pairing me with Ruth Madoc-Jones from the beginning and for pulling together such enormously talented people for the premiere. Thanks most of all for letting me make mistakes as I go. Bear with me, Yvette! I will earn what you've already given me.

Dreary and Izzy premiered at Native Earth Performing Arts, Inc. in November and December of 2005. The production was in association with Factory Theatre and played in the Factory Studio space. The company was as follows:

Isabelle Monoghan	Michaela Washburn
Deirdre Monoghan	Lesley Faulkner
Mrs. Harper	Sharon Bakker
Freddie Seven Horse	Ryan Cunningham
Director/Dramaturg	Ruth Madoc-Jones
Assistant Director	Clare Preuss
Set and Props Design	Camellia Koo
Costume Design	Joanne Dente
Sound Design and Composer	Lyon Smith
Fight Co-ordinator	Richard Lee
Stage Manager	Tamerrah Volkovskis
Assistant Stage Manager	Jennifer Lau
Production Manager	Stephen Lalande

• • •

Dreary and Izzy received its original workshop in the Weesageechak Begins to Dance XVII Festival for Native Earth Performing Arts at Buddies in Bad Times Theatre in Toronto, Ontario in October of 2004 with the following cast:

Isabelle Monoghan	Lura Merritt
Deirdre Monoghan	Michelle Latimer
Mrs. Harper	Colleen Williams
Freddie Seven Horses	Ryan Cunningham
Director/Dramaturg	Ruth Madoc-Jones
Stage Manager	Isaac Thomas

Thanks to Lorne Cardinal, Darrell Dennis, Diana Donnelly, Patricia Hamilton, Chapelle Jaffe, Craig Lauzon, Tamara Podemski, Sara Sinclair and Michelle St. John for reading roles at various stages of development. Thanks also to every person who auditioned for their contributions through playing with the script as actors.

•CHARACTERS•

ISABELLE MONOGHAN
DEIRDRE MONOGHAN
MRS. HARPER
FREDDIE SEVEN HORSES

•TECHNICAL NOTE•

Sound must come from localized area, not through the theatre's sound system. Real sounds must be used whenever possible. All pre-show and post-show music must be Canadian and suited to the 1970s, even if it is only heard in the lobby space. Careful attention must be paid to the props and set to evoke the correct time period.

I. Prologue – Isabelle inside

Lights up on ISABELLE, First Nations woman in her late twenties, simple hair style, black clothing.

ISABELLE Sometimes, somehow… this voice gets through. The one you hear right now. Level. Sensible. Able. It's not here all the time – I don't even live here. And yet she never doubts who I am, always knows she's heard from me before. Each time I slip into her head, she knows that I belong with her somehow. I try to find a way to fill the space where I should be. Gently. I begin. Sometimes it is hardly a whisper. Barely noticeable. Like a soft hello – she catches a hint of it, she has to still herself to make it out. This voice. Only when she rocks herself, all alone and quiet, does she hear the steady sound… of a smart girl. I would make her strong. Wise. And whole. The woman she could have been. I seep in through the cracks, insisting to be heard: Loud. Clear. Angry. So keen, so sharp that she feels pain and her body is taken. And she is lost—for a minute, five minutes, an hour—her whole body clutches, shouts and folds in on itself, suffering under the effort of trying to connect the Isabelle who exists with the Isabelle who cannot be. We fight each other, ourselves, this damaged brain, and I am newly broken, freshly wounded, to discover that I cannot come forward in a body that has seized. I can only exist when this body is well. She can't hear me without the pain of knowing what has been lost, taken… and so I stop. I leave her. I still myself until I am invisible again. And she goes back… out there, and I am deeper yet, inside. And she becomes herself again. The Isabelle you know.

We hear DEIRDRE's voice coming from the darkness, overlapping with ISABELLE's voice and in the background.

She is returned to the existing world.

DEIRDRE Izzy?

ISABELLE …and comforted by her sister.

DEIRDRE Come on, honey open your eyes.

ISABELLE   And everything is just as it was before.

DEIRDRE   Open your eyes, I'm right here.

ISABELLE   So it seems. But somewhere, she can feel that I was here…

DEIRDRE   You're here with me.

ISABELLE   I have to believe that she felt me. That I am more than just what's missing.

DEIRDRE   You're not going anywhere.

ISABELLE   They call it a seizure. And her sister smiles at me…

DEIRDRE   That was a big one, wasn't it?

ISABELLE   …if I stay quiet I can see her from deep inside. She tells me what a scare I've given everyone…

DEIRDRE   Can you hear me now, Iz?

ISABELLE   …and we carry on.

DEIRDRE   There you go. There's your big brown eyes.

ISABELLE   And it doesn't seem so terrible… because you'll never meet me – the Isabelle who sounds like this. Because I have never been born – was nearly erased, in fact, while in the womb. But I am felt – inside this damaged girl. I live inside the Isabelle you know. If you looked inside, you'd see where I am not. I am the holes in her unfinished brain. I am the lessons she will never learn. I am the conscience of this woman child, who will never know the crime that struck her down when she was still inside.

> *ISABELLE takes a deep breath as the blackness consumes her.*

ACT ONE

> *August 1975. Lights up on the Monoghan home. There is a living room with a hide-a-bed in earth tones, a coffee table, and side tables. One side table holds a lamp, phone, phonebook and address book, the other*

side table has a lamp and a paperback copy of Jonathan Livingston Seagull. *ISABELLE's room has a single bed, frilly with pink linens, a small white nightstand/ dresser with two drawers, a cup full of pencil crayons, a jewellery box [the kind with a ballerina inside] and a framed family photo. There are exits that lead to the kitchen, the bathroom, the basement and one that leads outside.*

II. Deirdre and Isabelle

DEIRDRE Monoghan, Caucasian woman in her late twenties, enters the living room. She wears funeral blacks. She sheds her purse, car keys, and jacket and sits wearily on the couch. She puts her arms on an armrest and rests her head upon them. ISABELLE, also in funeral wear, stands silently behind DEIRDRE, near the doorway. She is holding a few pencil crayon drawings and a pencil case. She looks about for a time, and then finally speaks.

ISABELLE Dreary.

ISABELLE waits for a response and then tiptoes toward DEIRDRE.

Dreary? You sleepin'?

DEIRDRE No, Isabelle. I'm not sleeping. I just sat down, for God's sake.

ISABELLE I called you. *(referring to the doorway)* Back there.

DEIRDRE What do you want, Izzy?

ISABELLE Was wonderin'. Where Mom is? *(read: Where's Mom?)*

DEIRDRE Izzy, do you remember where we were? Just now? Before we got into the car to come home?

ISABELLE Outside.

DEIRDRE Where outside?

ISABELLE   The park.

DEIRDRE   No. Not the park. A cemetery. Do you remember when I told you that word? Cemetery?

ISABELLE   Cemetery. Cemetery?

DEIRDRE   Yes. Cemetery.

> *ISABELLE nearly lies by answering "yes." She shakes her head instead.*

ISABELLE   No.

DEIRDRE   Come here, Izzy, so you're not staring at the back of my head.

> *ISABELLE walks around the side of the couch and remains standing.*

Cemetery. A cemetery is a place where dead people are buried. They—their bodies—get buried in wooden boxes deep in the ground and that is where they stay. Do you remember this?

> *ISABELLE tries to remember, but admits she cannot, shaking her head again.*

It's okay, Isabelle. Listen. Mom and Dad are dead now. Today we went to their funeral, which is the opposite of a birthday except that everybody only gets one. Do you remember opposites?

ISABELLE   Yes! Opposite is exactly what the other thing isn't. Happy / sad. Summer / Winter.

DEIRDRE   That's right. Birthday party / funeral.

ISABELLE   Oh. *(beat)* Birthday parties are fun.

DEIRDRE   Yes. And so what is a funeral?

ISABELLE   *(big breath, about to answer, exhale, big breath again)* Bored. Fun / bored.

DEIRDRE   Um. Yeah. Bor-ing. Can we say boring?

ISABELLE   Yes. Boring. Like at church.

DEIRDRE   Yes! Which is why funerals are partly at a church. Remember?

ISABELLE   Um. Yes.

DEIRDRE   Sit down with me Izzy – you're hovering.

> *ISABELLE sits down very close to DEIRDRE. DEIRDRE puts her arm around her, smiling at how endearing her sister is, in spite of her own fatigue.*

We had a funeral for Mom and Dad because they died. That means we won't see them anymore. Ever. Do you understand, Isabelle? Mom and Dad won't be in our lives anymore. But their memories go on forever. We can remember them and tell stories about them and look at their pictures... but they won't be here with us anymore. Do you remember any of this?

ISABELLE   I have to go swimming on Wednesdays at ten and what about lunch?

DEIRDRE   Well, there's lots of things—all of the things Mom and Dad used to do—that we have to do now instead. We still do everything we used to do, too, but now we do them all by ourselves and we don't get any help from them.

ISABELLE   How... wh... how will I get to swimming lessons?

DEIRDRE   Well, I'll drive you. But we have to take the station wagon because the Chevy was in the accident with Mom and Dad.

ISABELLE   My tapes are in the Chevy.

DEIRDRE   We'll have to get you some new tapes, Izzy.

ISABELLE   I want old new tapes. From when me and Mom go to garage sales.

DEIRDRE   We can go to garage sales together, okay?

ISABELLE   We can?

DEIRDRE   Yes.

ISABELLE   We can go to garage sales but not go swimming?

DEIRDRE   No, honey, me and you can go to garage sales. Not you and Mom. Me and you. No more Mom. Ever.

ISABELLE glares at DEIRDRE.

Don't look at me like that, Izzy, it's not my fault. I want to see Mom, too, but we can't anymore. I told you this already. I wish we could, too, but we can't. I'm sorry. It's not my fault. *(stops herself and tries to reframe but feels too frustrated)* Isabelle, you have no idea. You're such a friggin' idiot, you don't know how anybody else feels.

> *DEIRDRE immediately regrets her outburst and holds on to ISABELLE, too tight, as she fights tears. ISABELLE doesn't understand why DEIRDRE is so worked up. She waits until her sister's breathing calms and then asks...*

ISABELLE   Dreary, are you very mad?

DEIRDRE   No. I'm sorry.

> *ISABELLE waits as patiently as she can while DEIRDRE breathes deeply, calming herself. ISABELLE pats her rhythmically, absentmindedly on the back.*

ISABELLE   What is the opposite of presents?

DEIRDRE   What, hon?

ISABELLE   If at a birthday you get presents, what do people get at a cemetery?

DEIRDRE   At a funeral. What do they get at their funerals?

ISABELLE   Yeah.

DEIRDRE   Well, Izzy, they don't get anything. What's the opposite of getting?

ISABELLE   *(to herself)* What's the opposite of getting. Getting. Getting a present. I'm going to get a present. *(beat, to DEIRDRE)* Taking a present?

DEIRDRE   No, love. Giving. At your funeral, you give away everything you ever got. Because you won't be using it anymore. Everyone who knows you gets your things.

ISABELLE   Does Mom and Dad give me any of their things?

DEIRDRE   Yes. You get all of their things, Isabelle. Everything. And I get you.

> *DEIRDRE and ISABELLE look at each other a moment. DEIRDRE stands up and so ISABELLE does, too. DEIRDRE wants to walk away, but she doesn't.*

Okay, honey. Come on. Time to get changed. I can't look at you in that colour anymore. Doesn't suit you.

> *DEIRDRE pulls off ISABELLE's charcoal sweater, revealing a cheery coloured t-shirt beneath. ISABELLE leans on DEIRDRE's shoulders as her skirt is pulled down by her sister, revealing white cotton panties and striped knee-highs.*

ISABELLE   How come I get everything?

DEIRDRE   *(beat)* Because you're the oldest.

ISABELLE   Then how come you get me?

DEIRDRE   Because I'm trying to get canonized. What do you want for supper?

ISABELLE   Those sandwiches on the foldie tables at the basement at the church.

DEIRDRE   Can't have those. Alpha-Gettis?

ISABELLE   Alpha-Gettis. When we're going to watch TV?

DEIRDRE   Why, what's on?

ISABELLE   Shows.

DEIRDRE   We're taking the day off from TV. Out of respect.

ISABELLE   'Kay. When you're going to make me the Alpha-Gettis?

> *DEIRDRE looks at ISABELLE for any trace of willful cheekiness and sees only curiosity.*

DEIRDRE   I'm making them now. If you stop asking questions. You go grab your PJs first. Put them on in here.

ISABELLE M'Kay.

> *ISABELLE hums "Amazing Grace" as she fetches her PJs from her room and then returns to the living room to put them on. DEIRDRE does her thing in the kitchen and comes out to tidy the living room of ISABELLE's things. The microwave beeps.*

DEIRDRE Don't know what we ever did without a microwave oven.

> *DEIRDRE grabs the supper and returns to ISABELLE.*

Okay, Rascal, here we go. Steamin' hot Alpha-Getti.

> *ISABELLE shows DEIRDRE her clasped hands. DEIRDRE does the same. ISABELLE waits until DEIRDRE starts… this is the routine.*

In the name of / the Father and of the Son and of the Holy Spirit. Amen.

ISABELLE —the Father and of the Son and of the Holy Spirit. Amen. Thank you, God for the delicious meal and for allowing us to share it as a family. We are blessed and ever thankful for your bounty. In the name / of the Father and of the Son and of the Holy Spirit. Amen.

DEIRDRE —of the Father and of the Son and of the Holy Spirit. Amen.

> *Immediately after crossing, ISABELLE attacks the bowl, eating voraciously.*

ISABELLE Freshie. Cherry Freshie.

DEIRDRE You can have a drink when you finish eating.

> *ISABELLE stops eating and puts on a grumpy face.*

What?

ISABELLE My throat. I can't swallow if it's so dry.

DEIRDRE I'm not putting up with this crap, Isabelle. You get a drink when you're done, or else you fill up on that disgusting sugar water and you're hungry again in twenty minutes.

>ISABELLE *makes a show of choking on her Alpha-Getti.*

Okay, that's enough. Go to bed right now.

>ISABELLE *eats quietly.*

No. It's too late. Go to your room.

ISABELLE   You ain't Mom!

DEIRDRE   I am now. Get your ass in there.

>ISABELLE *is stunned that DEIRDRE said "ass." She gasps and covers her mouth.*

You heard me. Go.

ISABELLE   You said it. I telling.

DEIRDRE   Oh, yeah? Who are you telling? Hm? Get up.

>ISABELLE *is too shocked to resist. She giggles and allows herself to be led into her bedroom.*

ISABELLE   Could I say it?

DEIRDRE   I don't care, Isabelle.

>When they arrive at her bed, ISABELLE *forgets she is being punished and climbs into bed happily.*

ISABELLE   Goodnight, Dreary.

DEIRDRE   Goodnight.

>DEIRDRE *returns to the living room and tidies angrily, deeply frustrated and suppressing a world of emotion. She sits on the couch, trying not to break down, nearly swearing to herself.* ISABELLE *waits for an opportunity to plea for respite. Finally...*

UGGHH!

ISABELLE   Dreary, I not tired.

DEIRDRE   Too bad! You should have eaten your supper.

ISABELLE   I was gonna. *(beat)* Maybe if I stay up ten more minutes, if I may.

> *Beat.*

DEIRDRE   Get back out here, Izzy.

> *ISABELLE returns to the couch and puts her head on DEIRDRE's lap.*

Isabelle, you have to be good because I'm already fed up. I've had to do a lotta terrible things since Friday. Okay?

ISABELLE   'Kay. You're sad, Dreary?

DEIRDRE   Yes.

> *ISABELLE strokes DEIRDRE's cheek. DEIRDRE tries to smile at ISABELLE.*

Do you have all of your things ready for swimming? It's tomorrow, you know.

ISABELLE   Yes, I'm ready 'cause I love swimming.

DEIRDRE   I know you do. You're a little turtle. You can swim and walk, just like a turtle.

ISABELLE   I had a dream of a turtle. It was big and I got to stand on her, like a bird on a elephant.

DEIRDRE   That sounds like fun. Did it move while you were standing on it?

ISABELLE   She walked. Yes. Dreary, will you still go to the university?

DEIRDRE   Maybe someday. We have to figure out lots of things first. Things about you and me and... how things will work around here.

> *They sit in silence.*

ISABELLE   Dreary, maybe I can be sleepy.

DEIRDRE   Yeah? I'm pretty pooped, too. Let's get you to bed then, okay, sweetie? Make sure you're not tired out for swimming. We have to make sure we aren't late again, like we were for the doctors'. People will think we can't do this.

ISABELLE   Like that retard, Dr. Lizée.

DEIRDRE   Isabelle!

ISABELLE   What?

DEIRDRE   You don't call people retards.

ISABELLE   Other people say "retards." I heard a grown-up say "retard."

DEIRDRE   Well, we don't use that word.

ISABELLE   Dr. Lizée always says we can't do stuff.

DEIRDRE   She says a lot of stupid things, it's true. Even so. She wouldn't say "retard" and neither do we.

> *DEIRDRE leads ISABELLE back to her bed and tucks her in.*

ISABELLE   What about brusheen my teeth?

DEIRDRE   Too much work. We'll do them first thing in the morning.

ISABELLE   Ho-ly.

DEIRDRE   Goodnight, little turtle, see you in the morning.

ISABELLE   Goodnight, Dreary. Love you.

> *DEIRDRE turns to leave…*

ISABELLE   *(half asleep)* Dreary, whaddabout my story?

DEIRDRE   Too tired, hon. We'll do two tomorrow. Say your prayers.

> *ISABELLE crosses herself and prays silently, moving her mouth.*

ISABELLE   Amen.

DEIRDRE   G'night.

DEIRDRE returns to the living room. She removes her black sweater, revealing a camisole. She undoes her skirt and lets it fall to the ground, leaving her slip in place. She folds her sweater and then remembers something and trots back to ISABELLE's room.

Izzy. Isabelle, do you have to go to the washroom first? Isabelle? Hey! Do you need to pee?

ISABELLE shakes her head.

Are you awake right now, or are you just answering "no" out of habit?

ISABELLE   Awake.

DEIRDRE   Okay. Goodnight. Sweet dreams. *(She is compelled to stay. She sits down on ISABELLE's bedside.)* The little girl was happy all the time. She didn't ever feel sad or lonely or miss anyone. She smiled when other people cried, and she forgave people before they knew they were sorry. *(beat)* Love you.

She kisses ISABELLE on the head, and returns to the living room. She stretches out on the couch, pulling the throw blanket over her legs. She puts her feet on the coffee table and stares blankly, thinking of her parents. In an effort to distract herself, she finds her book and stretches out with it. She lets the book fall to the floor and holds herself tight. She crosses herself and silently prays for strength, weeping quietly. She buries her face in the cushion. The lights dim and both girls seem to settle in to sleep. ISABELLE suddenly sits up in bed. She throws her blankets off the bed, onto the floor.

ISABELLE   Yeah. Washroom.

She exits and snaps on the bathroom light. We hear her pee and flush the toilet and then we briefly hear the shower. She kills the light and returns to bed, soaked to the skin, and wiping her hands on a tiny towel. She climbs back onto her bed, with only the towel as a blanket. Touch black. Silence.

III. Apple Jacks

*Lights warm to daytime levels. DEIRDRE snaps
awake. She checks her watch.*

DEIRDRE Shoot. Okay. Ten minutes to eat breakfast, hour to
digest, fifteen to get to the pool, ten to get her into her
swimsuit, five in the shower… yes. We can do this. Izzy!
Wake up, we gotta get you to swimming lessons! Ow, *(her
neck)* bugger!

> *DEIRDRE rushes to the kitchen and returns to the
> living room with two bowls of cereal. She puts them on
> the coffee table.*

Come on, Isabelle, get up and eat your breakfast and take
your meds! You have to have them before you swim, and
you have to eat with them, so get up. Now! Apple Jacks,
Izzy! Come on!

> *DEIRDRE goes to the kitchen again and returns with
> two cups of orange juice. She sets them down beside the
> bowls.*

Isabelle! It's morning. Wednesday morning, time to go
swimming! Nothing is ever easy with you, for heaven's sake,
woman, you make me crazy.

> *DEIRDRE goes to ISABELLE's room. She sees
> ISABELLE trembling and wet.*

Isabelle. What did you do? My God, you're drenched.
Where's your – your… why didn't you use your blankets?
My God, you're soaked through, Izzy.

ISABELLE Mom? Mom, I din' pee the bed, I got up. By myself.

DEIRDRE Good girl.

> *DEIRDRE finds the blankets and wraps them around
> ISABELLE, helping her out of the wet clothes as she
> keeps her warm in the blanket.*

Oh, geez. You're all hot. What do I… I'll be right back, okay,
honey? Isabelle?

> *DEIRDRE eases ISABELLE onto the bed gently and runs into the living room. She picks up the address book and flips through it frantically.*

Okayyyy… let's see. No, no. Hm.

> *She picks up the phone and dials a number. A phone rings.*

MRS. HARPER 'Mornin!

DEIRDRE Hello. Mrs. Harper? This is Deirdre Monoghan.

> *Light up on MRS. HARPER, Caucasian semi-retired woman. She wears a colourful housedress and has her hair partly in curlers. Though she is not ready for the day, she does wear bright red lipstick. She holds a spatula and the phone receiver.*

MRS. HARPER Hi, Deirdre. How are you girls?

DEIRDRE I'm okay, how are you guys?

MRS. HARPER Just fine sweetheart, just fine. Now, how is Isabelle adjusting?

DEIRDRE She's doing all right for that, but actually the reason I was calling you was to ask something about her health.

MRS. HARPER Oh, Jesus! Is everything okay?

DEIRDRE I'm sure she'll be fine. It's just – she spent the night without blankets and I guess she had her window open and now she's really shivering and wet and feels pretty hot. I'm sorry to bug you, but I know you're a nurse and I wondered if you could come by, maybe or—

MRS. HARPER Oh, I'm sure she just caught a chill, Deirdre. Just wrap her up and give her lots of fluids. Keep an eye on her and she'll be just peachy.

DEIRDRE Okay, it's just, you know, she has these sort of seizures, she always has.

MRS. HARPER Right, Deirdre. Seen her in emerg once or twice. Now, have you got the Dilantin she takes for it?

DEIRDRE   Well yes, but you know, it's not exactly like epilepsy. Sometimes when she feels off, she just—

MRS. HARPER   Okay, hon, here's what you need to do. Take her temp and see that it's not more than one-oh-two; that'd be the time to worry. Get her taking her meds and make sure she eats with 'em, give her plenty of fluids – you're the best girl for the job, mind.

DEIRDRE   All right. Should I take her to a doctor?

MRS. HARPER   Oh, no. No point bothering with one of those fools. Unless you have a woman doctor, have yeh?

DEIRDRE   Well, yeah. Isabelle sees Dr. Lizée every month. We missed her regular check-up last Monday, so we're going next week. *(beat)* I just – I mean, I can't keep an eye on her every—

MRS. HARPER   I'm sure this has been hard on her, missing her mother and all, you just be a good friend to her and trust that everything will work out.

DEIRDRE   Yes, Mrs. Harper. I will.

MRS. HARPER   Take a good look at yourself, Deirdre, honey. Your mother wouldn't have left you with Isabelle if she didn't think you could handle it. You're the only sort of mother she has now, so you've just got to make a go of it, okay? See if you can't figure out you can do it. Better than losing your sister along with your folks.

DEIRDRE   Yeah. Absolutely. Thank you Mrs.—

MRS. HARPER   Must run, Deirdre. Gotta get Ken's breakfast in him and get to Super Sam before the soaps start. Don't be a stranger, now dear. You call anytime, anywheres. Take care of you girls, okay?

Light out on MRS. HARPER.

DEIRDRE   Okay. Bye, Mrs. Harper. I'll ca – Mrs. Harper? Mrs... are you?

DEIRDRE holds the receiver in her lap a moment. She listens to the dial tone, out of sheer need. She sets it in

> *her lap again, looking into it. Finally, she hangs it up. She returns to ISABELLE's room.*

Come on, up you get. *(big sigh)*

> *She pulls ISABELLE out of bed, blankets and all.*

Up! Good girl. Come now, over to the living room, just while I make the bed, okay? Shhh. That's it. Watch your head, hon.

> *She settles ISABELLE onto the couch, returns to the bedroom and strips the bed of wet linens. She returns to the living room because she hears ISABELLE whimper and softly say...*

ISABELLE   Mom... Mom? Mom...

DEIRDRE   *(defeated sigh)* Isabelle...

> *ISABELLE wakes slightly and looks up at DEIRDRE.*

ISABELLE   Dreary. Why I'm on the couch? We camping here?

DEIRDRE   Yes, Isabelle. We're camping in the living room.

ISABELLE   Where are you're sleepin'?

DEIRDRE   I don't know. On the floor, I guess. I'll pretend it's the ground, and you got the air mattress again.

> *ISABELLE notices DEIRDRE's exhaustion and suspects she is the cause of it. She rolls onto the floor.*

ISABELLE   Here, Dreary, you get the mattress 'cause I din' help even put up the tent.

DEIRDRE   You're a crazy girl, Izzy. Come on, you'll sleep in your bed.

ISABELLE   No. *(sweetly)* I don' want to.

DEIRDRE   Well, you're not sleeping there. It's dusty. We haven't vacuumed in ages. Come on.

ISABELLE   *(full charm on)* No, Dreary, I want to sleep out here with you. We can make the couch big and it be a bed for two people. Like camping with a really big air mattress.

*DEIRDRE relaxes and decides to enjoy her sister
instead of feeling put out by her.*

DEIRDRE   Okay. Sit over there, out of the way.

*ISABELLE scoots over as DEIRDRE moves the coffee
table and changes the couch into a sofa bed.*

How do you feel?

ISABELLE   Cold. Hot. I dunno.

DEIRDRE   Do you feel sick?

ISABELLE   Maybe. Maybe a little. Do I have a cold?

ISABELLE puts a finger up her nose.

DEIRDRE   No. Fingers out.

ISABELLE   Do you?

DEIRDRE   No, I don't. I'm just a little tired.

*ISABELLE looks around and notices the sunshine out
the front window and the cereal bowls on the coffee
table.*

ISABELLE   It's morning time.

DEIRDRE   Yep. Come on up. We can try to find some cartoons.
Do you feel like eating cereal?

ISABELLE climbs onto the sofa bed.

ISABELLE   Yes.

DEIRDRE   Okay, I'll get us some new bowls. These ones have
gone soggy. So drink your orange juice for now.

ISABELLE   Dreary can I have Apple Jacks?

DEIRDRE   Yes, you can.

ISABELLE   Dreary are you mad at me?

DEIRDRE   No.

DEIRDRE exits to the kitchen.

ISABELLE   Mom. Mom? MOM! MOM! Where did she go? It's only morning time.

> *DEIRDRE re-enters with two new bowls of Apple Jacks.*

DEIRDRE   Why were you calling Mom, Izzy?

> *She climbs onto the bed, giving one bowl to ISABELLE and draping a dish towel around her neck.*

ISABELLE   Where's my real bib?

DEIRDRE   It's in the wash. So be careful, this isn't the same as a real bib.

ISABELLE   Well, I see that. This goes on the cupboard door.

DEIRDRE   Yes, you would think that's all it does.

> *ISABELLE clasps her hands. DEIRDRE starts them off.*

In the name of / the Father and of the Son and of the Holy Spirit. Amen.

ISABELLE   —the Father and of the Son and of the Holy Spirit. Amen. Thank you, God for the delicious meal and for allowing us to share it as a family—

> *ISABELLE opens her eyes.*

Hey. Dreary, where Mom is?

DEIRDRE   Where do you think she is, Isabelle?

> *Beat.*

ISABELLE   The store?

DEIRDRE   Yeah, sure. The store.

ISABELLE   What she's getting there?

DEIRDRE   Apple Jacks, you moron.

ISABELLE   But we have Apple Jacks.

DEIRDRE   Yeah, well. I guess she doesn't know any better 'cause she's dead.

ISABELLE   Oh, yeah.

DEIRDRE   Dad, too.

ISABELLE   Whoa… Dad never goes to the store.

> *DEIRDRE bursts out laughing causing ISABELLE to start and spill her Apple Jacks on herself.*

DEIRDRE   I'm sorry, Isabelle. Oh, I'm so sorry but you're so funny. Crap, I can't believe you sometimes. Oh, God, it's all over you. Let's put you in the tub, okay?

> *ISABELLE nods. They go to the bathroom, we hear them run a bath.*

IV. Come In

> *The doorbell rings. DEIRDRE hurriedly throws some clothes on as she moves to the door.*

DEIRDRE   You stay there, I'll get it. Now, when you turn the taps off, turn off the red one first, and then the blue one, okay? So you don't get hurt. I'll be right back. Don't duck under, I'm not washing your hair right now.

ISABELLE   Well, but who is it?

DEIRDRE   It's probably another lady with a casserole.

ISABELLE   NOOO!

> *DEIRDRE laughs. She answers the door.*

DEIRDRE   *(stunned, and a bit too loud.)* Hi.

FREDDIE   *(offstage)* Hi. How are you today?

DEIRDRE   Good. Do we know you?

FREDDIE   Ah, nope. My name's Freddie. I'm here on behalf of Vac-U-E-Z vacuums and I'd like to offer you a free demo of our incredible product.

DEIRDRE   Oh. Okay. Come in.

FREDDIE   (o/s, surprised) Thank you.

> FREDDIE SEVEN HORSES, First Nations man in
> his late twenties, has an easy manner, confident, well
> educated, but a little down on his luck lately. He's a bit
> off his game, but still sociable. He wears a dress shirt
> and tie with neatly pressed pants and well shone shoes.
> He carries a large bulky vacuum in a brown cover.

DEIRDRE   You can leave your shoes on.

FREDDIE   Oh. Thanks.

DEIRDRE   As you can see, it hasn't been vacuumed in awhile.

FREDDIE   Well, then, I came at the right time.

DEIRDRE   Yup.

> DEIRDRE leads FREDDIE straight into the living
> room and alongside the bed. She notices him look at it,
> and she is suddenly embarrassed.

So, you say you do demos?

FREDDIE   That's right. Ah – we want you to see how well the
product does, and we're quite certain that it will sell itself. If
you want more information about the machine after the
demo, I'm happy to answer any questions, but on the whole,
these vacuums tend to sell themselves.

DEIRDRE   Really? So you must have about a dozen of these out
in that little car of yours, huh? To keep up with demand?

FREDDIE   Huh. No, ma'am. Just the one. When a vacuum is
purchased, it's ordered straight from the factory and
delivered to your door, brand new. You can pick a colour to
match your home.

DEIRDRE   Great. Uh – would you help me?

FREDDIE   Oh. Sure.

> They put the hide-a-bed back to bed mode.

DEIRDRE   Okay, then.

FREDDIE   Okay.

> *FREDDIE uncovers the vacuum and unwinds the cord.*
> *He unpacks some of the attachments.*

Do you have somewhere I can plug it in?

DEIRDRE   *(laughing)* Sorry. This is like a bad Barbara Cartland book or something – you come in, and BOOM there's a bed, then you're all like. "Do you have somewhere I can... plug it in?" Heh, heh... sorry.

> *DEIRDRE is embarrassed by her own joke. She takes*
> *the cord from him and plugs it into the wall.*

FREDDIE   Okay. So, this is the power switch here... *(loudly, though scarcely audible over the vacuum's roar)* You'll find that the bag capacity is really quite impressive. You'll change it a lot less often than you would with the vacuum you have now. It also has a lot more strength. You're not gonna tear a hole in it if you accidentally suck up a nail or a screw

> *DEIRDRE moves the coffee table and points out a spot*
> *that needs attention. She checks him out as he*
> *vacuums.*

Thanks. A lot of older houses have that really short carpet, or even rugs on wood floors, and this will be great on those too, but where it's really impressive is on these long shag rugs that everyone's getting. Where most vacuums would only get the surface dirt and particles, this one really digs deep and gets right down to dust and small molecules, without damaging the carpet itself. Would you like to try?

> *He offers her the vacuum. She puts her hands up and*
> *shakes her head, mouthing "I'm okay."*

It's indispensable in kids' rooms, where the dirt can be a serious problem and lead to stuffy noses, and colds and stuff. Do you have any kids?

> *DEIRDRE senses he is not talking vacuum talk and*
> *breaks out of her staring reverie.*

DEIRDRE   Pardon me?

FREDDIE   Kids. Do you have any children?

> *DEIRDRE shakes her head vigorously and points at her*
> *wedding finger – no ring. He nods and smiles,*
> *understanding. She smiles back at him.*

ISABELLE   Dreary! Dreary! My hands are becoming old. *(beat)*
Dreary! I'm out now.

> *ISABELLE stands in the bathroom doorway with*
> *a towel wrapped around her, her hair wet in places.*
> *DEIRDRE quickly herds her into her bedroom.*

DEIRDRE   Let's put some clothes on you before you come out,
okay? We have a visitor.

ISABELLE   Is that a boy vacuumeen our house?

> *FREDDIE turns off the vacuum and admires his job.*
> *He quickly checks his hair and glances toward the*
> *bedroom.*

FREDDIE   Yeah, so I met this great chick. Oh, yeah? What
happened? Well, she invited me in to her place and I, uh –
I vacuumed her living room. Cool.

ISABELLE   Who is that boy, Dreary? Why he's vacuumeen our
house?

DEIRDRE   Here you go… put that on. Arms up. Good girl. Your
hair is wet.

ISABELLE   Not all. I was only splasheen.

DEIRDRE   All right, put your socks on and come out and meet
him, okay?

> *DEIRDRE returns to the living room, where*
> *FREDDIE is wrapping up the cord.*

I'm awful, I forgot my sister in the tub. Whoops!

FREDDIE   You look after your little sister?

DEIRDRE   Yeah. Well, big sister, but really she's mentally not
much older than eight or nine.

FREDDIE   Oh. Is she – has she always been like that?

DEIRDRE   Yeah. She – nobody really noticed until she couldn't get past grade five or so, but… yeah.

FREDDIE   Yeah? I have a cousin like that. People are weird around him – you know? Like they're embarrassed, or something. They don't quite look right at him.

DEIRDRE   I like your voice.

> *FREDDIE is surprised, then he looks like he might kiss DEIRDRE. She wants him to. He snaps out of the moment.*

FREDDIE   So… what do you think?

DEIRDRE   Uh – oh! Good. Nice. I mean, we haven't cleaned up in here in ages, and it looks pretty good now. Thank you.

> *ISABELLE enters, hair still damp and sticking up in parts.*

ISABELLE   Hi. My name is Isabelle. Dreary is my sister and this is my house. Why you're vacuumeen in my house?

> *FREDDIE shakes ISABELLE's hand, and she keeps holding it.*

FREDDIE   Hi. I'm Freddie. I was vacuuming because I sell vacuums.

ISABELLE   Really? How many?

FREDDIE   Um. Not too many yet, but it's only my first week. It's a new job.

> *FREDDIE gently wriggles his hand out of ISABELLE's grasp, and she takes the hand nearer to her instead.*

ISABELLE   Are you always going to vacuum my house?

FREDDIE   No. Just today, to show your sister how good the vacuum is.

ISABELLE   Is it pretty good, Dreary?

DEIRDRE   Yeh. Pretty good.

ISABELLE *(to FREDDIE)* You look nice. *(back to DEIRDRE)* Is it better than our new vacuum from Sears?

FREDDIE You have a new vacuum?

ISABELLE Yes. In the Sears catalogue I got new runners and Dreary got three panties for one forty nine and Mom got a new vacuum for the house.

FREDDIE Your mom got a new vacuum?

DEIRDRE Yeah. But she doesn't live here anymore.

ISABELLE She went to get Apple Jacks.

DEIRDRE Izzy, let go of Freddie's hand.

ISABELLE But I was holdeen it.

DEIRDRE Yes, I know, but he has to get back to work.

> DEIRDRE *rolls the vacuum to the door, SR, where she fusses with the cover.* ISABELLE *follows* FREDDIE *to the door, standing as close as possible.*

FREDDIE So, I guess if you already have a new vacuum and the vacuuming has been done… I can get going. Unless you want me to do the rumpus room or something.

DEIRDRE I didn't – buy that other vacuum. I just – sorry about that.

ISABELLE We already have Apple Jacks. But Mom doesn't know any better 'cause she's dead and so did Dad.

DEIRDRE Leave him alone, Izzy.

ISABELLE Are you a Indian?

DEIRDRE Isabelle!

FREDDIE Yes, I am. Well, my mom is Native and so I'm half Native.

ISABELLE You say your Indians "Native"?

FREDDIE Yep.

ISABELLE How come?

FREDDIE 'Cause we're not from India. Neither are you. So you should say "Native."

ISABELLE I'm from Canada.

FREDDIE Right.

ISABELLE Right!

FREDDIE *(laughs)* And so are your ancestors – that's what Native means. It means your people have always lived here.

ISABELLE Native. My mom is Native, too. But not the dead one, the other one. And probably she has more kids, too, but I don't know them.

DEIRDRE Isabelle—

FREDDIE It's okay. It's nice to meet you, Isabelle. Maybe you can phone me if you ever need a vacuum.

FREDDIE gives ISABELLE a pamphlet.

ISABELLE *(pleased)* Oh.

FREDDIE Right there. See? That's me. Freddie Seven Horses.

ISABELLE I'm Isabelle but no horses. Plus the Chevy was in the accident.

FREDDIE takes the vacuum from DEIRDRE.

DEIRDRE I – I didn't mean to… I don't talk to grown-ups much. Sorry.

FREDDIE So, she's adopted?

ISABELLE Adopted. Native.

DEIRDRE Yeah. My mom wasn't supposed to be able to… yeah, they adopted her, and then they had me, so…

FREDDIE So,… you live here alone? Just you and Isabelle?

DEIRDRE Yeah. They… don't worry about it. We lost them last week. They were in an accident.

FREDDIE looks at ISABELLE, recalling her "dead" comment from a moment ago.

Yeh.

> *FREDDIE looks at ISABELLE again, who is staring at him inappropriately and feeling the material of his shirt. He absentmindedly takes her hand to prevent her from grabbing something she shouldn't.*

FREDDIE   I'm sorry. What happened?

DEIRDRE   My dad was driving and he had a stroke and they happened to be crossing the river just then—

FREDDIE   Oh, last week crossing the Old Man river—

DEIRDRE   Yeah.

> *ISABELLE hums "Old Man River" (Kern/ Hammerstein II) for a moment and then smiles at her memory of doing that every time they drive over the bridge.*

FREDDIE   Oh, God, I saw that in the paper. I'm so sorry. *(He can't think of anything to express how sorry he is.)* I – that... that's really awful.

DEIRDRE   Yep.

FREDDIE   I'm really sorry. Um. Take care.

> *FREDDIE squeezes ISABELLE's hand and leaves. DEIRDRE watches after him. ISABELLE hugs DEIRDRE.*

ISABELLE   Dreary, you like him.

DEIRDRE   No, cutie. I don't even know him. I like you.

ISABELLE   Dreary, I want to go to bed, even though it's daytime.

DEIRDRE   Well, that's okay. You're allowed. You're a sickie because you threw your covers away last night.

ISABELLE   I did?

DEIRDRE   Yep.

ISABELLE   How come?

DEIRDRE   Because you're not right in the head.

They laugh and go to ISABELLE's room.

ISABELLE   Dreary, if our mom is dead, can I have my Native mom?

DEIRDRE tucks her sister in.

DEIRDRE   No, Iz, you can't. You already know this, my heart. Your Native mom was very sick. She was so sick that she died because she couldn't get better.

ISABELLE   I'm sick, too.

DEIRDRE   You're only a bit sick, Isabelle. You're not gonna die. Lay down and get some rest now, so you'll get better even faster, okay?

ISABELLE   Dreary, is it okay if I go to bed without my Apple Jacks?

DEIRDRE   Are you hungry?

ISABELLE   No.

DEIRDRE   Well then it's okay. You can have something when you get up again. Now try to keep your sheets on. I'm going to tuck you in tight so they stay, okay? You're gonna be like a little sausage.

ISABELLE   No, a pig in the blanket.

DEIRDRE   Okay. An Izzy-pig in a blanket. Goodnight, Isabelle.

ISABELLE   Good morning-night.

DEIRDRE   Good morning-night.

DEIRDRE starts to leave and then stops.

Isabelle... I don't mean to be mean to you. I'm just a little tired.

ISABELLE   You should have a nap, Dreary.

DEIRDRE laughs lightly.

Do I have to say my prayers if it ain't night?

DEIRDRE   No, it's okay, hon.

ISABELLE   Bless Mom bless Dad make Dreary not sad! (*She laughs.*)

DEIRDRE   I love you, Izzy.

ISABELLE   And you love Freddie.

DEIRDRE   Shut up and go to sleep.

> *ISABELLE laughs and then does her own prayer to herself. DEIRDRE returns to the living room and trips on a vacuum attachment as the doorbell rings. There are more attachments on the couch.*

Oh, my God. Holy crap.

> *She answers the door.*

(*offstage*) Hi. I'm sorry – I packed up your vacuum and forgot about the extra piece, and the other parts…

FREDDIE   (*offstage*) Yeah, the attachments, yeah.

> *They enter and start gathering the attachments, bumping into each other and accidentally touching hands now and then – moments charged with electricity.*

DEIRDRE   Here, let me—

FREDDIE   Got it. Thanks.

DEIRDRE   Whoops. Oh, here—

FREDDIE   Thank you. Sorry, there's one wedged under the cushion there.

DEIRDRE   Oh, there you go.

FREDDIE   Thanks.

DEIRDRE   Is that all of them?

FREDDIE   Yeah, I think so.

DEIRDRE   Well, if we missed any, you know where we live. You can always come back for it tomorrow if you have to.

FREDDIE summons his courage and sets an
attachment deliberately on the couch.

FREDDIE   Okay.

FREDDIE gauges DEIRDRE's reaction, who blushes
and smiles.

Your mom didn't buy you a vacuum salesman at Sears, did
she?

DEIRDRE   No.

FREDDIE   Where did Isabelle run to?

DEIRDRE   She went to bed. She's not really feeling well.

FREDDIE   Don't you – I mean, you're looking after her by
yourself? Is there someone in your family who could help
you out a bit or something?

DEIRDRE   No. Not really, no. It's not – so bad. It's only been –
not long, just for a week so far. But… yeah.

FREDDIE   Hard?

DEIRDRE   Can be.

FREDDIE   Well, I think that's… you're pretty… *(amazing)* uh –
I don't have a ton of friends here anymore. Lived in Toronto
for awhile. Came back, and don't really… the people I used
to know… it's kinda like they're mad at me for leaving. Even
though I've come back.

DEIRDRE   Toronto? Wow…

FREDDIE   Mm. U of T.

DEIRDRE   Cool. I mean… that's a drag. I got in to University
but I can't go 'cause I'm, *(She gestures to the surroundings.)*
well – I'm here now. I'm all she has, really, and… well, it was
in their will that I should…. Not that I'd – I mean, it's only
the University of Lethbridge, who cares? But she doesn't –
she thinks everything's normal.

He moves closer to her. They stare at each other.

Uh… what did you take?

FREDDIE   Theology. I'm gonna come by tomorrow. After work.

> *She steps closer to him.*

DEIRDRE   Okay. Do you wanna have supper? We've got all these casseroles...

FREDDIE   Sure. Thanks.

> *DEIRDRE takes a step toward FREDDIE. He does the same. She extends her hand and they shake hands. They laugh uncomfortably.*

Maybe I'll try kissing you tomorrow.

> *She nervously forces a small laugh and walks toward the door. He follows.*

You remind me of the girl I was in love with in grade two. She broke my crayons on the first day of school, and I knew I'd have to marry her. Melanie Woodhouse. Didn't work out though. I told her she was pretty and she said I was gross.

> *FREDDIE slowly and lightly kisses DEIRDRE. He is clearly more experienced than she.*

ISABELLE   *(softly, sleeping)* Amen.

FREDDIE   Isabelle... she calls you Dreary.

DEIRDRE   Yeah. She couldn't say "Deirdre" for ages – so everyone called me that until she realized they were kind of making fun. It came back when we were teenagers.

FREDDIE   Deirdre.

DEIRDRE   Monoghan.

FREDDIE   Deirdre Monoghan.

> *He shakes her hand again. They laugh.*

FREDDIE   See ya tomorrow.

DEIRDRE   'Kay.

> *He exits with vacuum in tow.*

V. Sink or Swim

DEIRDRE breathes it out calmly until FREDDIE disappears from view. She then squeals and has an excited freak out, dashing to ISABELLE's room.

DEIRDRE   Isabelle. Izzy! *(ISABELLE does not stir, DEIRDRE is dying to talk to someone. After some time she speculates...)* I wonder if Sears would take that vacuum back?

A beat. DEIRDRE hugs the sleeping ISABELLE who is barely stirring. DEIRDRE runs out, returning with an armload of laundry, to which she adds the wet towel. She exits and we hear a washer being employed. DEIRDRE returns and sits on ISABELLE's bed again. ISABELLE moves her face toward DEIRDRE but stays asleep. DEIRDRE walks over and gazes down the hall toward the front door. She is nervous for tomorrow.

I have no idea what I'm doing. *(loudly)* Is anybody home? Okay. Settle down.

DEIRDRE goes to the phone and picks up the receiver and address book: thumbing through, she eventually dials, desperate. Light up on MRS. HARPER, who is dressed now, her hair done, and lipstick in place. She is eating the last of a pink snowball.

MRS. HARPER   Hello!

DEIRDRE   Hello, Mrs. Harper? It's Deirdre again. How are you?

MRS. HARPER   Just fine, sweetheart, how is Isabelle?

DEIRDRE   Oh, she's okay after all. Just maybe a chill, like you said.

MRS. HARPER   Good to hear.

DEIRDRE   Yeah. I just wanted to call and thank you for your advice, and sorry to trouble you.

MRS. HARPER   Not a worry, Deirdre.

DEIRDRE   Listen, Mrs. Harper, I know we haven't really seen a lot of each other since you guys moved, and I wondered do you want to come over for coffee sometime?

MRS. HARPER   Oh, now you listen here. You don't have to feel you need to repay me for anything, Deirdre, it was just a bit of advice. Not a trouble at all.

DEIRDRE   Oh, no, I'd love to have you. I don't really have any friends. My age. And we have all of these squares and cakes and things that people brought by, just crowding our whole kitchen...

MRS. HARPER   Oh, that sounds shit-sweet, Deirdre. Why don't I come by after "Days," then.

DEIRDRE   Oh. Today?

MRS. HARPER   Sure, hon.

DEIRDRE   Okay. That's perfect. I'll thaw some things out. We'll have a sweets buffet and some coffee.

MRS. HARPER   Why don't we make it Irish, hey, honey? I'll bring some of Ken's rye with me and have him drive me over and then pick me up once we're good and liquored.

DEIRDRE   Oh. Sounds good.

MRS.HARPER   Good then, we'll see you after "Days." Bye for now.

DEIRDRE   Bye.

> *Light out on MRS. HARPER.*

Serendipity-do-dah. Hey, Isabelle, we're gonna have another visitor. Dizzy Izzy? You must be sick. *(feels her forehead)* Poor thing. You're still warm. See if I can find that thermometer.

> *DEIRDRE returns with a thermometer. She puts it in ISABELLE's mouth and waits awhile.*

The little girl was very smart and very sweet. She was the very best one at hide and seek – she hid her smart behind her sweet so barely anyone could see. Unless they wanted to.

(beat) There must be some tangled wires in that head of yours. You're so pretty. Poor baby.

ISABELLE Dreary?

DEIRDRE Yes, my heart?

ISABELLE What dat in my mouf?

DEIRDRE Thermometer. I'm checking your temperature.

ISABELLE Ain't we s'posed to put it on the light bulb?

DEIRDRE No. That's just what I used to do so I could miss school. Learned it from comic books – Jughead did it.

ISABELLE *(giggles)* Jughead. That boy going to come back?

DEIRDRE Yes, he is. He's going to visit us tomorrow. We'll go to the store in the morning and then we'll see Freddie at night, does that sound good?

ISABELLE Good. *(beat)* Dreary, when is it Wednesday again?

DEIRDRE It's Wednesday today, Izzy.

ISABELLE When I'm going swimming at ten?

DEIRDRE Oh, Izzy, you couldn't go today because you're sick.

ISABELLE Shut up. *(She lets the thermometer drop from her mouth.)* Yes I am so going swimming at ten.

DEIRDRE Isabelle, I need to you to stay calm and be good. Ten o'clock is passed. You can't go swimming when you're sick. If a sick person goes to the pool, she'll make everyone else sick. And she'll get sicker, too.

> *ISABELLE thumps DEIRDRE and gears up for a big tantrum – like a three years old's tantrum, unrestrained and visceral.*

Ah! Stop it, Isabelle. Stop it right now. Shhhh. Shhhh. It's okay, love. Calm down.

> *ISABELLE jumps out of bed and starts flailing and acting out.*

ISABELLE   I hate you! You're a bastard, you stupid dummy! I hate your guts, you SHUT UP you! AHHHHH!

> *ISABELLE runs into the living room with DEIRDRE pursuing, trying to gently physically calm her.*

DEIRDRE   Shhhhhh… that's okay honey, you settle down now. It's okay. I didn't mean to make you mad, but you can't go swimming when you're sick.

ISABELLE   Unhhhhhh. AHHHH! Why you're so MEAN, Dreary? Why you're so mean to meeeee?

> *ISABELLE pushes DEIRDRE away. DEIRDRE stops following her.*

DEIRDRE   Shh, honey, calm down. Calm down, Izzy. Shhhhhh…

ISABELLE   Why you won't let Mom take me swimming?

> *She looks into the kitchen trying to find her mom.*

ISABELLE   Mom? Mom!

DEIRDRE   Okay, now settle down. Stop it right now. That's enough. *(ISABELLE wails.)* Isabelle, you need to take some breaths. Isabelle. Look at me. Calm down and take some breaths. Okay?

> *ISABELLE sits herself on the floor, rocking slightly. DEIRDRE carefully approaches her.*

Good. Okay? Are you okay?

> *ISABELLE punches DEIRDRE hard.*

ISABELLE   Shit on you!

DEIRDRE   Ow! Holy crap!

ISABELLE   I hate you hate you hate you! Go away! Get away! Shit on you! Why my moms are dead? Uhhhhhhh…

DEIRDRE   I don't know why, Isabelle. Sometimes life is shit, and you just have to wait for it to get better. Eventually, if we just keep on going and doing regular things, it'll seem normal.

ISABELLE   But I din' get to go swimming. You wouldn't let me go.

DEIRDRE   Ah, Isabelle, I didn't want you to miss swimming. *(DEIRDRE bends down next to ISABELLE, both of them sitting on the carpet. DEIRDRE rubs ISABELLE's back.)* You got sick in the night, and it's just because I fell asleep by accident on the couch and we slept in. I'm sorry. I should have checked on you, but how was I supposed to know you'd get in the shower after you went pee? You don't do normal things, I can't guess what you're gonna do.

ISABELLE swats limply at DEIRDRE's arm.

Hey. What did Mom say about hitting?

ISABELLE hangs her head.

Huh? What did she say?

ISABELLE   *(mumbling)* Hug, don't hit.

DEIRDRE   I can't hear you, what was that?

ISABELLE   HUG, DON'T HIT!

DEIRDRE   That's right. Hug don't hit. Now, who was hitting someone just a minute ago.

ISABELLE   ME!

DEIRDRE   That's right. Sounds like you've got some residual anger there, Izzy. You wanna punch a pillow for awhile? *(ISABELLE eyes her suspiciously.)* It's okay to hit a pillow, just not people.

ISABELLE   Pillows. *(DEIRDRE nods.)* Pillows not people.

DEIRDRE   Yeah. Now you got it. Hug, don't—

ISABELLE   Hit.

DEIRDRE   Pillows, not—

ISABELLE   People.

DEIRDRE   Right. So, do you want to punch a pillow, or do you feel better?

>*ISABELLE lunges at her sister, hugging her.*

Love you, Dizzy Izzy. Oh, honey. Good girl. Hug don't hit.

ISABELLE   Hug don't hit.

DEIRDRE   Do you want to have a sleepover in the living room tonight?

ISABELLE   Yes. With pajamas and chips.

DEIRDRE   Okay, my heart. Let's get your pajamas on.

>*ISABELLE bounces around a bit, perfectly content now. DEIRDRE goes to ISABELLE's room to fetch pajamas. She returns with some plaid flannel pajamas.*

ISABELLE   No! No, I don' wan' wear thoooose!

DEIRDRE   Isabelle, what's wrong with you? You said you want pajamas.

ISABELLE   Want the pretty ones.

DEIRDRE   Your pink ones?

ISABELLE   Yeah.

DEIRDRE   Okay, okay. I'll get your baby dolls. I'll have to turn up the heat, I hope you know.

>*DEIRDRE finds the pink frilly baby doll pajamas. While she's gone, ISABELLE stretches out and then spins around with her arms over her head.*

Okay, get undressed and put these on.

>*ISABELLE stands staring at DEIRDRE.*

What? These aren't them?

ISABELLE   No. But you can't just watch me when I take off my panties and everything.

DEIRDRE   Oh, come on. Suddenly you're shy? Well, then go change in the bathroom. I have to put your blankets on the hide-a-bed; you're not kicking me out. Not unless you wanna do it yourself.

ISABELLE rolls her eyes and scoffs, DEIRDRE imitates her.

The nerve of some people. Jeepers.

She sets up the sofa bed and ISABELLE returns in her pretty pajamas. She prances about, doing "ballet."

Whoa, beautiful ballerina. Oh my goodness, you're so graceful, Isabelle. I feel like I should call you Miss Isabelle.

ISABELLE   Okay.

DEIRDRE   Woooo, Miss Isabelle, you are so enchanting. Okay, let's find some chips you like and finish the bed.

ISABELLE   I find some chips by myself?

DEIRDRE   Sure.

ISABELLE   Goody goody gum drops, goody goody gum drops... *(trails off as she runs into the kitchen)*

DEIRDRE   Don't mind me. I'm just the help.

ISABELLE   Dreary, you put on your jammies, too!

DEIRDRE   Okay.

DEIRDRE leaves to change into PJs ISABELLE returns with animal crackers, a clear bag of plain Old Dutch potato chips from the two bag box, and some chocolate chip cookies.

ISABELLE   Dreary? Where you went?

DEIRDRE   *(offstage)* You told me to put my PJs on.

ISABELLE finds it hilarious that DEIRDRE obeyed an instruction she gave her.

ISABELLE   You – you put on your pajamas right now!

DEIRDRE   Okay, very funny. *(She returns.)* There. Better?

ISABELLE   No, you put on some pretty pajamas, too.

DEIRDRE   Miss Isabelle, you're the magical dancer. We can't have two magical dancers. I'm the bed maker.

ISABELLE   Oh.

DEIRDRE   Okay. Do you want to sit in bed and see if there's a movie on?

ISABELLE   Yes.

> *ISABELLE jumps onto the sofa bed, crushing the snacks. ISABELLE and DEIRDRE gasp.*

My chips! And my cookies!

DEIRDRE   It's okay, hon. We'll just have to chew them less. Here.

> *Trying to clean up, ISABELLE spills crumbs all over the bed.*

ISABELLE   Sorry, Dreary.

DEIRDRE   Oh, it's okay, Izzy. Don't cry over spilled crumbs, right?

ISABELLE   Right.

> *ISABELLE brushes the crumbs to the carpet.*

DEIRDRE   No, don't... ah... crap. We need another boy with a vacuum to come over.

ISABELLE   Yeah.

> *The doorbell immediately rings. ISABELLE is amazed.*

He came back.

VI. Mrs. Harper

> *Having forgotten about MRS. HARPER, DEIRDRE nervously hopes it is FREDDIE again. She answers the door.*

DEIRDRE   Mrs. Harper! Come in.

MRS. HARPER   You didn't tell me it was a pajama party, Deirdre Monoghan. Jesus Christ, I could'a wore my pink baby dolls.

MRS. HARPER carries slippers and her own mug.

MRS. HARPER   Hi there, cutie pie. How the hell are yah?

ISABELLE   Good.

DEIRDRE   Isabelle, you remember Mrs. Harper who used to live across the street? She used to make you cookies all the time.

ISABELLE   Yes.

MRS. HARPER   Sure she does. *(ISABELLE hugs MRS. HARPER.)* Oh, there you go. I used to pull your slivers out, too, darlin', do you remember that? My God, but she'd holler and bellow. Your mother couldn't bear to cause her the pain, but they have to come out, so over she'd come to mean old Mrs. Harper.

DEIRDRE   Isabelle had a bad mood there for a minute, so I pulled out the bed in case she might just fall right asleep afterward. We're having a camp out with chips and pajamas.

MRS. HARPER   Well, lets get it goin'. Did you make us that coffee?

DEIRDRE   I will do that now. Isabelle, do you want to show Mrs. Harper the drawings you did at the cemetery?

ISABELLE   Yes.

> *ISABELLE bounds over to her room, and pulls some drawings from under her bed, lining them up on the floor. MRS. HARPER hands DEIRDRE a small bag with a mickey of rye and a can of spray whipped cream.*

MRS. HARPER   Bugger was too skint to share, but he bought us a little one of our own. Don't be thrifty with it, it's all ours.

DEIRDRE   Okay. Do I still put milk in?

MRS. HARPER   I brought some whipped cream there. Two sugars for me, hon.

> *DEIRDRE leaves to the kitchen, reading the whipped cream can. MRS. HARPER joins ISABELLE who is on her bed, looking down at the drawings.*

What an *artiste* you are, Isabelle honey.

> *ISABELLE giggles throughout this scene.*

How the hell did you draw such pretty flowers? And look at that graveyard – it's like I'm there! And that crazy scarecrow.

ISABELLE   That's Dreary, cryin'.

MRS. HARPER   Are you sure? *(ISABELLE nods.)* Why don't we put these on the wall, huh? You got any tape? *(ISABELLE nods.)* Well, go fetch, sweetie and we'll display this exhibit.

> *ISABELLE runs to the kitchen to get the tape from DEIRDRE while MRS. HARPER takes a closer look at the drawing of DEIRDRE. ISABELLE runs back.*

You want them here, above your bed? Or beside your bed?

> *ISABELLE lays on her bed, testing the angles.*

ISABELLE   Put it on that wall, 'cause if it's on this wall and when it falls, and I'll get a paper cut eye.

MRS. HARPER   Well, you don't need that. Christ, you have enough problems, don't you, hon?

ISABELLE   Yep.

> *MRS. HARPER hangs the pictures. ISABELLE hums "Jesus Loves the Little Children" (traditional).*

MRS. HARPER   Arright. There you go. Good?

ISABELLE   Yes. Thank you. Let's go show Dreary.

MRS. HARPER   All right. You go do that and I'll meet you back in the living room.

ISABELLE   'Kay. Go!

> *ISABELLE runs back to the kitchen, and MRS. HARPER settles herself in the middle of the sofa bed. She eats some crumbs from the bedspread. DEIRDRE and ISABELLE enter with paper plates full of assorted squares, coming in on either side of MRS. HARPER.*

DEIRDRE   Here's a bit of everything, Mrs. Harper. All sorts – Nanaimo bars, date squares, little tarts.

ISABELLE   Lots of sweets, but be careful 'cause if you have too much you'll get really really riled up and then really really cranky after that.

MRS. HARPER   Well, I feel like an emperor. All I need is a dancing girl.

> *ISABELLE quickly sets down her plate on the bed and resumes her ballet.*

DEIRDRE   I'll grab our coffees, Mrs. Harper.

MRS. HARPER   Aw, Pete's sake, call me Mo.

ISABELLE   Your name is a boy's name, Mo.

MRS. HARPER   Well, darlin', it's Mo for Maureen. Now sit yourself down before you make me dizzy. Come here. Have some chocolate. It's good for you.

ISABELLE   I like those ones.

MRS. HARPER   Really? The matrimonials?

ISABELLE   Some people call them date squares.

MRS. HARPER   Yes, they do. But I call them matrimonial squares. And anyone who has them has to get their palm read first. So, put your hand out. No. The other one.

> *DEIRDRE returns with big Irish coffees. Intrigued by the prospect of palm-reading, she sets them on the coffee table*

DEIRDRE   Will you do mine too, Mrs. Harper?

MRS. HARPER   Sure.

ISABELLE   Me first. Her name is Mo now.

DEIRDRE   Bossy.

MRS. HARPER   Okay. Huh. Barely any lines. But you got the ones that count, anyway. Looks like you'll live long enough. Long enough to be happy about your life, but not quite so

long that you're happy you're dyin'. That's just about right,
I'd say. Wouldn't you?

ISABELLE / DEIRDRE   Yes. / Sounds good.

MRS. HARPER   Okay. Doesn't look like you'll get married, but
that doesn't mean you won't have lots of cute guys in your
life, you pretty thing.

DEIRDRE   She has a boyfriend at swimming.

MRS. HARPER   Really?

ISABELLE   Yep. Devin. He jumps from the high board and he
has clown hair. Like this. *(ISABELLE swirls her hands around
her head.)* But when he jumps in his hair goes pfffff… and
sticks down.

DEIRDRE   Big head of red curly hair.

MRS. HARPER   Redhead. Is he hot tempered, Isabelle?

ISABELLE   No. *(giggling)* I touched his penis in the pool.

MRS. HARPER   Oh!

DEIRDRE   Our mom had to have a meeting with his mom one
time because they were caught messing around in the deep
end.

ISABELLE   *(still laughing)* Messing.

DEIRDRE   It's not funny, Isabelle.

MRS. HARPER   You be careful, Isabelle. You can't trust boys.
Especially the cute ones. Okay? Okay. *(MRS. HARPER draws
back.)* Oh. I'm usually pretty good at this, but…

DEIRDRE   What?

MRS. HARPER   Looks like one baby.

ISABELLE   I have a baby?

DEIRDRE   No, you don't. And you won't. That must mean
a puppy or something. Izzy's been begging for a puppy ever
since we were little.

MRS. HARPER *(unconvinced)* Yuh. That could be it. The lucky pup to get you would be like your baby, wouldn't it?

ISABELLE I like babies.

DEIRDRE You're not having babies, Izzy. You're a baby yourself.

MRS. HARPER Do you see this line, Izzy?

ISABELLE Yes.

MRS. HARPER It means you will always love, and will always be loved. You lucky girl.

ISABELLE See Dreary's now.

MRS. HARPER Okay. Looks like you'll be breaking world records with your lifespan, Deirdre.

DEIRDRE Oh, great.

MRS. HARPER What is it you call your sister again, Isabelle?

ISABELLE Dreary?

MRS. HARPER Exactly. Don't be so gloomy, hon, it could be worse. Too long a life beats the hell out of passing on as young as my Josephine.

DEIRDRE Sorry, Mrs. Harper. I didn't mean it.

MRS. HARPER Uh. Never mind. Let's see about marrying you off to some rich lawyer, okay? Yep. Looks like you'll have a husband. Or at least the love of your life. Nothing to sniff at. And money – that's two for two.

DEIRDRE Good thing. I could never keep a job with that one around.

MRS. HARPER Sure you did. You were at FasGas for awhile there, and Kresge's before that.

DEIRDRE Yeah, but I always ended up missing shifts or coming late 'cause of her, and then I'm fired.

MRS. HARPER Is that so? Shame, huh?

ISABELLE Any babies like me?

DEIRDRE   You're my baby, Isabelle.

ISABELLE   Uhn-uh. I'm older than you are.

MRS. HARPER   *(She knows this.)* Are you, dear?

ISABELLE   Yes. Almost one whole year.

MRS. HARPER   According to this, you're gonna have two. Whether that includes I-s-a-b-e-l-l-e or not I don't know.

ISABELLE   Isabelle!

DEIRDRE   Wow. A husband and two kids. I've never thought that far ahead.

MRS. HARPER   Well, it could be sooner than later. Are you goin' with anyone right now?

ISABELLE   I go with her everywheres.

DEIRDRE   She means do I have a boyfriend, Isabelle.

ISABELLE   She never has a boyfriend. Only me. *(read: only I do)*

MRS. HARPER   No dancing around a thing, is there?

DEIRDRE   Hm. Nope. That's not exactly true, though. Izzy just thinks if she wasn't there, it didn't happen. I dated this guy from work once, at FasGas. But then he got fired before I did and I couldn't be bothered to make the effort to see him outside of work.

MRS. HARPER   Oh, and so few are worth the effort, eh?

DEIRDRE   Yeah. Then another time, in college, I dated this guy from my English class. But I was only there for three and a half months. Plus. I always have to make sure this one is running on schedule. Takes up all my time.

MRS. HARPER   Pass us those coffees, Izzy.

DEIRDRE   One at a time, Iz.

MRS. HARPER   And did you get to know these boys… quite well?

DEIRDRE   Uh – fairly well. The one guy Jeff, was really fun but we didn't really have all that much to talk about. And then

Byron was pretty cute, but we didn't ever get to... well... he only ever had his car to hang out in, and... well, it was kind of cramped and awkward. So, technically, I guess I'm still... ugh, God...

MRS. HARPER   A virgin?

ISABELLE   Like Mary.

> *MRS. HARPER laughs, DEIRDRE is embarrassed.*

DEIRDRE   Barf. That word. It's like "leper."

MRS. HARPER   Oh, hon. There's nothing wrong with having standards.

DEIRDRE / ISABELLE   I guess. / Um hm.

MRS. HARPER   And, you're not yet thirty, so no need to panic. You should look at getting yourself out a bit more, though. Spend time with people your own age.

DEIRDRE   Yeah. I've never really had girlfriends to talk about stuff with, you know? And my mom... we never... well I'm pretty sure my dad was her only – uch, I can't even imagine bringing that up with her.

MRS. HARPER   Remember – I'm a nurse. I'm not squeamish and I never been shy. If ever you want to talk about any of that—even the basic mechanics, you know—there's a lot goes along with it – you call Mo and we'll go shopping and just have a day, okay?

DEIRDRE   Kay. Actually... there is this guy—

ISABELLE   Dreary likes Freddie.

DEIRDRE   This guy came to the door today—

MRS. HARPER   Like a missionary?

DEIRDRE   No no no! This really gorgeous guy.

MRS. HARPER   And did you get his name?

DEIRDRE   Yeah. Freddie. He gave us his pamphlet.

ISABELLE   Me his pamphlet.

DEIRDRE Anyway, he's a vacuum cleaner salesman and he came in and did his demo. I kind of misled him, just because he's so gorgeous and he was really sweet. We just got a new vacuum, and he found out, so I can't believe he wasn't miffed at me for letting him vacuum my friggin' living room.

ISABELLE Dreary, you said Mom and Dad said in that letter that it's my house.

DEIRDRE So, he's coming over for supper tomorrow and I'm nervous because, well, I'm not exactly... I've never even had the house to myself before.

MRS. HARPER Aw, Deirdre, if he vacuumed your rug, vacuum salesman or not, he's sweet on you. You'd be amazed what it can take to make a man put his own dirty ginch in the hamper, never mind vacuum the rug.

DEIRDRE Do you think I'm crazy, having him here for our first date?

MRS. HARPER Well, if you'd rather go out, you can send Isabelle over to mine and you two can go to the show.

DEIRDRE Hm. Maybe... nah, I think that would be harder. It's nice to have Izzy around because she breaks the ice and really makes people honest. Thanks, though. Maybe if we get past this date I'll take you up on that.

ISABELLE Me and Freddie are both Natives. You guys are white.

MRS. HARPER This boy is an Indian?

DEIRDRE Yeah. He says "Native." He's so smart. And nice. And so... sexy. He has this smile that absolutely makes you want to... wow. And his skin just looks so soft and... *(big breath)* ...edible.

MRS. HARPER What do you know about him?

DEIRDRE Well... he's really polite, he works hard at his job, he's so good with Izzy, he just moved back here from Ontario—

MRS. HARPER From Kingston?

DEIRDRE *(missing the inference)* Uh, no. Toronto. For University. A lot of his friends are kind of annoyed with him for ever moving there for some reason. And he reads the paper.

MRS. HARPER If this boy grew up here, there's a good chance he'll know who Isabelle's relatives are. They're like that, the Indians – they all know each other. Did youse ever find out a last name for her?

DEIRDRE They don't tell you that. Not even the birth mother's first name. You get some papers, but that sort of thing is blacked out.

MRS. HARPER I s'pose if you're signing your babies away, you don't much care what becomes of them.

DEIRDRE My dad figured she had other kids before Izzy, 'cause I guess she was in her forties when she had her.

MRS. HARPER Oh, I'm sure she does. Only people who seem to have more babies than the Mormons. I wonder how much – like her they are, you know?

DEIRDRE Yeah, that's just it. My dad was sure she's this way because her mom was an alcoholic, but the doctors wouldn't say yes or no about that.

MRS. HARPER Cowards. I've seen babies come out from the womb, stinking of wine. Most babies smell sweet, right off the bat. You know that sweet cookies and milk smell that babies have? But these wine soaked babes – they're always so tiny. And how they cry – the worst hangover you ever seen. And the trembling. Poor things. You can't tell me wine is okay for a pregnant woman.

ISABELLE What happen to the babies, Mo?

MRS. HARPER Sometimes, if they're lucky, they have a family who can take care of them. If they have a family who's patient, able to handle it, they do okay. They become beautiful young people for the rest of their lives. Always young, always a child. It's for the best, really. So they don't know what they're missing. I can't imagine the heartache of knowing you've been robbed. It's a crime. To take that future from them before they've even known to miss it. And you know, you might not believe it to hear it, but rich ladies can do the very same. Even doctors' wives, for Christ's sake! Probably why we pretend it doesn't happen. Call them hyperactive, or blame it on candy or TV. Christ. Listen to me. What a lousy drunk I am. Party pooper! I tell you what. I'm gonna leave you girls to your party and I'm gonna come back for a visit every Wednesday from now on. What do you think?

ISABELLE   I could draw more pictures.

MRS. HARPER   Then I'll have to come by and hang them up!

ISABELLE   Yeah.

DEIRDRE   We would love to have you over. Every Wednesday. We'll eat these squares until they run out and then we'll make some more.

MRS. HARPER   Good. Help me up, honey, I gotta see a man about a horse before I hit the road.

ISABELLE   Freddie has seven horses.

MRS. HARPER   Good catch, Deirdre. (*MRS. HARPER exits to the bathroom.*)

DEIRDRE   Will you be okay with hanging out with me and Freddie tomorrow, Izzy?

ISABELLE   Yes. I like him. And he's pretty.

DEIRDRE   What do you think of Mrs. Harper? Would you like to hang out at her house some time?

ISABELLE   Okay. I hope she uses the right towels.

> *ISABELLE hovers near the bathroom door.*

We're not supposed to use those little ones, or Mom gets mad.

DEIRDRE   Isabelle, those are guest towels, so she can use them if she wants to. And anyway, they're Mom's guest towels. She's not going to have guests anymore, so now they're just regular towels.

ISABELLE   Regular using towels?

DEIRDRE   Yeah. We can use them if we want to.

ISABELLE   Okay.

> *ISABELLE knocks on the bathroom door.*

MRS. HARPER   *(offstage)* Out in a sec!

ISABELLE   I was going to tell Mrs. Harper she can use those towels but then I didn't. She'll be out in a sec.

DEIRDRE   Isabelle, why don't you gather up some of those sweets and wrap them on a paper plate for Mrs. Harper? She can take some home with her.

> *ISABELLE does a terrible job of pretending she can't hear DEIRDRE.*

Just some of them, Izzy. We can keep most of them for us. Go on.

ISABELLE   *(sulking)* Okay.

> *ISABELLE goes to the kitchen and MRS. HARPER returns.*

MRS. HARPER   Well, thanks for the coffee, hon. You make them real good – with a lot of kick; Ken will find I'm a little feisty when I get home. Hope he's rested up!

> *They laugh.*

DEIRDRE   Mrs. Harper – Mo, can I ask you something really personal?

MRS. HARPER   Course you can. What is it?

DEIRDRE   Am I pretty? I mean, if you were me, would you be embarrassed to take your clothes off with a man?

MRS. HARPER   Oh, honey. You're just an absolute doll. You've got yourself the sweetest smile and a lovely slim figure. I've never been the petite type, so if I were you, I'd be sweeping the driveway naked, whether it needed it or not. Now, listen, honey. If you're ready to give your body to this boy at some point, you make damn sure he deserves you. There's all sorts of men out there, and you don't really know this boy yet. And if you're not ready for a baby, you get yourself on the B.C. Pill and get him to pick youse up some rubbers. I don't know all the ins and outs of you Catholics, but I know you won't want to find yourself with an unwanted baby, no matter what the Pope says about rubbers and so forth. Make sure it's what you want – it's true what they say, your first you'll remember forever.

DEIRDRE   I know. I just met him.

MRS. HARPER   But if you feel good about him, well you trust yourself. If you want to have a good time, and his intentions are clear, you have a good time. But don't be bringing an unwanted baby into the world. God knows there's too many of them as it is. Okay?

DEIRDRE   Okay. Thank you, Mrs. Harper.

> *MRS. HARPER hugs an emotional DEIRDRE.*

MRS. HARPER   Oh, now. Don't you worry about a thing. You'll do wonderful. Just wonderful. With all of it. Now. Stop your blubbing and I'll see you next week, arright? Now, if Ken calls, just tell him I needed the walk, so as not to worry about fetchin' me. I'm dyin' for a smoke, but he doesn't let me have them. I allow myself one every day and bull to those who'd keep me from it. *(shouting o/s)* Take care now, Isabelle!

> *ISABELLE enters with a paper plate of goodies covered with cellophane.*

DEIRDRE   Isabelle, those are all butter tarts.

ISABELLE   *(with genuine disgust)* With raisins.

MRS. HARPER   Oh, you're a hoot, Isabelle Monoghan. Whups. Fetch my mug, there, hon. *(ISABELLE grabs MRS. HARPER's mug.)* Make sure this boy is the sort you want around before you trust him too much, okay? You don't really know – his family and such, you know? Where he's come from. Okay. Thank you for the tarts, my dear. And we'll see you next week, too.

ISABELLE hugs MRS. HARPER.

Oh, you girls are so lovely. Take care, now. See yuhs.

ISABELLE   *(as if from a distance)* Bye!

> *DEIRDRE walks MRS. HARPER out and ISABELLE goes over to the sofa bed, sprawling out across the width of it, on her stomach and facing DS. She is very sleepy. DEIRDRE returns.*

DEIRDRE   She is so cool.

ISABELLE   They all know each other.

DEIRDRE   What, hon?

ISABELLE   Mo says the Indians all know each other.

DEIRDRE   Oh. Yeah…

ISABELLE   How come they don't know me?

> *DEIRDRE can't answer. ISABELLE drifts to sleep. DEIRDRE covers her with blankets and checks her forehead.*

DEIRDRE   Poor thing. We better take you in to the clinic tomorrow. *(beat)* I guess I won't be able to budge you 'til morning. Ah, well, my bed's more comfortable than this thing anyway. Even if I don't have a bedroom to put it in. *(beat)* Suppose I could use the master bedroom. *(She thinks about the process of going through her parents' things.)* I'll be in your bed, Iz. Sweet dreams.

> *DEIRDRE climbs into ISABELLE's bed. ISABELLE stirs. Her back arches as she grimaces slightly. She makes a small sound, as if in a nightmare. She clenches up her muscles all at once. ISABELLE seizes, making only small choking and grunting sounds, drooling and twitching, her eyes rolling and fluttering, groping at the blankets. The seizure intensifies and then eases. She stops and lies quietly.*

> *Blackout. End of Act One.*

ACT TWO

VII. My Sister's Barf

A warm morning wash rises on the living room.
DEIRDRE enters, dressed for the day. ISABELLE still
rests silently on the sofa bed.

DEIRDRE   Get up, Izzy! We have to go to the store before lunch,
'cause we're going to the doctor's. Up you get, sleepy bum.
Hey, wiener. Better get up or I'll tickle monster you. Holy,
someone's really tired out. Izzy, you sleep like the dead.

>   *She uncovers ISABELLE, and sees vomit on the*
>   *mattress.*

Isabelle! Isabelle, you got sick, honey, are you all right?
Isabelle. Isabelle, can you hear me? Isabelle!

>   *DEIRDRE lightly smacks ISABELLE on the face,*
>   *opening her eyelids, etc.*

There you go, wake up, honey. Come on. Come on now, we
gotta go to the doctor right now, okay, Isabelle? Good girl,
come on.

>   *DEIRDRE pulls ISABELLE off the sofa bed, carrying*
>   *her like a child, front to front, ISABELLE's legs*
>   *around DEIRDRE, just awake enough to hold on*
>   *slightly.*

Oh, honey, you're okay. You're okay. We have to get you
some meds right away, okay? They'll give you some at the
hospital.

>   *DEIRDRE exits, carrying ISABELLE. She quickly*
>   *returns for her purse and car keys, and exits again.*
>   *A moment passes – time moves from morning to late*
>   *afternoon. Knocking is heard offstage. More knocking.*
>   *A doorbell.*

FREDDIE   Hello? Deirdre? Isabelle? Hey, the door is open, so
I'm coming in.

FREDDIE enters, with the vacuum. He has removed his tie and wears a different dress shirt.

Hello? Are you guys hiding or something? The lights are on. Hello?

He notices the vomit.

Deirdre? Are you guys okay?

He looks in ISABELLE's room and into the bathroom. He goes to the kitchen and returns with a dishtowel. He cleans up the vomit and gathers up the sheets, piling everything on the floor. He changes the bed to a couch.

Hello!

He checks his watch. He spots the crumbs from the chips on the carpet. He grimaces. Glancing around, he stands, checking out the front door to see if anyone is coming. He unwraps the vacuum and unwinds the cord. He swings the end of the cord around like a lasso, but at crotch level.

(phony cowboy voice) Hey, do you have anywhere I can, uh... plug this in? *(recalling his embarrassment)* "Your mom didn't buy you a vacuum cleaner salesman at Sears, did she?"... Idiot.

He vacuums up the crumbs. The phone rings and he wonders if he should answer it. It rings for some time, so he finally does answer. Light up on MRS. HARPER in her small space, a full head of curlers, housedress and red lipstick, coffee cup in hand.

Hello, Deirdre and Isabelle's... can I help you?

MRS. HARPER   For Pete's sake, who's this?

FREDDIE   I'm a friend of—I was just—Freddie.

MRS. HARPER   Oh, Freddie. The one for Deirdre. Okay, Freddie, can I speak with Deirdre, if you please?

FREDDIE   Well, it looks like they ran out for a minute. The lights are all on and the door was open – I mean wide open, but nobody's here. I came in because I thought they were here.

MRS. HARPER   You let yourself in?

FREDDIE   W—

MRS. HARPER   Isn't that strange. Did you check the backyard?

FREDDIE   No. I – I just finished work early, so I came by, and the door was open, and there's like, puke on the hide-a-bed, so I cleaned that up and folded the—

MRS. HARPER   You say you found vomit, hon?

FREDDIE   Yeah. The hide-a-bed was pulled out, and someone threw up on it. I know Isabelle felt sick yesterday...

MRS. HARPER   That's right. Listen, Freddie, you call St. Mike's and I'll call the general, and I'll call you right back. But check the yard before you call.

Light out on MRS. HARPER.

FREDDIE   Well they might just be – hello?

FREDDIE hangs up the phone and finds the phonebook, locating the hospital's number and reaching for the phone as it rings. Light up on MRS. HARPER.

Hello?

MRS. HARPER   Yep, hon. The girls are at the general – in emerg. I'll meet you there. I'm the one with the curlers in. Bye, now.

FREDDIE   I... *(Light out on MRS. HARPER.)* I really don't know them very well. Fuck.

He starts to pack up his vacuum, but leaves it.

Fuck it.

A moment of empty stage. Time shifts to early evening. Enter DEIRDRE followed by FREDDIE carrying ISABELLE "newlywed" style. She is sleeping and wrapped in a small blanket from the car.

DEIRDRE   Sorry about the mess. I left in a hurry and I didn't really have time—

FREDDIE   Sorry. I came in 'cause the door was open, and I saw... um, the bed was open. So I cleaned it up, but I don't know if you have a washer or whatever.

DEIRDRE   You cleaned up my sister's barf?

> *DEIRDRE stares as he walks past her and carries ISABELLE to her room and tucks her in.*

What's with you?

FREDDIE   What do you mean?

DEIRDRE   Well... this. And the puke. And the... general niceness. What are you doing? Are you an orphan or something? Don't you have your own family?

FREDDIE   Yeah, I have my own family. But I like yours.

DEIRDRE   My sister's a retard and I'm the only other person.

FREDDIE   At least half your family's nice to me.

> *FREDDIE packs up his vacuum. DEIRDRE is feeling disempowered, frustrated.*

DEIRDRE   You vacuumed?

FREDDIE   Why are you angry with me?

DEIRDRE   Why are you here?

FREDDIE   Because you have sad eyes. Because you smell incredible, and I feel important when you look at me. I like how dorky and rude you are and how much you love your sister. I like that she's Native but you don't feel like that separates you two at all. I like that you weren't afraid to let me into your house. Although that was pretty stupid of you. And I like how your hair is kind of crazy.

DEIRDRE   It's not crazy.

FREDDIE   Can I stay? 'Cause I don't want to leave, and I don't think you want me to either.

DEIRDRE   Why don't you like your family?

FREDDIE   I like them. I just don't like being there too much. I'm too old to be back living at home. I feel like I'm in high school again. I'm gonna get an apartment as soon as I sell two more vacuums.

>   *A beat as they decide what's next. FREDDIE walks over to the couch. DEIRDRE slowly follows, rounding the other side. They sit.*

DEIRDRE   How many have you sold?

FREDDIE   Three.

DEIRDRE   In a week?

FREDDIE   Yeah.

DEIRDRE   Seems like a lot.

FREDDIE   It's not bad.

DEIRDRE   I forgot to give Izzy her pills. She had a seizure, maybe more than one. I let her sleep on the hide-a-bed 'cause she was sleeping so hard. I just forgot about them 'cause she was sick all day. I just forgot.

FREDDIE   My mom has diabetes. She forgets her insulin all the time. We have to remind her. One time, she forgot my Dad already reminded her, and so when I reminded her again, she took more and then she had too much insulin. It was pretty bad.

DEIRDRE   I'm sorry. *(beat)* The doctor thinks Isabelle would do better in a loony bin. She kept saying that. I get called in to identify my parents' bodies and the first thing our doctor says is that I should "think about arranging for Isabelle's care." Like someone else should be looking after her just because my parents are gone. Like I wasn't there with Izzy every single month for her check-ups. Brought her to her appointments, ever since I could drive. Get her prescriptions, take her to swimming...

FREDDIE   What do you think? *(DEIRDRE doesn't know what he's asking.)* About the loony bin?

DEIRDRE   Ugh – they always say that. Ever since we were eight or nine, they try to get us to send her away. She's the only friend I've ever had. It's always been – me and Izzy. I can't imagine not having her around.

FREDDIE   I'm sure they'd take you, too.

> *Beat. They both laugh at how inappropriate the remark was. Laughter fades and sexual tension takes over again.*

DEIRDRE   You're unusual.

> *FREDDIE leans over and kisses DEIRDRE. He sits back to gauge her reaction. She looks like she might eat him.*

I was supposed to go to the doctor's at four.

FREDDIE   Are you okay?

DEIRDRE   Yeah. I wanted to go on the birth control pill.

FREDDIE   W-what?

DEIRDRE   The birth control pill. I haven't… I've never… been on the pill before.

FREDDIE   Oh.

DEIRDRE   I've never had sex before. I mean, I've done stuff, but never actual sex.

FREDDIE   Oh.

DEIRDRE   Is – is that… a problem?

FREDDIE   No. I mean, not for me.

DEIRDRE   Good. Because – cool.

> *Big silence.*

Just thought I'd… make sure. Just in case. Sorry.

FREDDIE   So… do I get the grand tour?

DEIRDRE   Actually, the clinic is open late on Thursdays.

FREDDIE   I'm sorry... what?

DEIRDRE   The clinic. It normally closes at five. But on Thursdays, it's open 'til nine.

FREDDIE   Just like the mall.

DEIRDRE   Yeah.

      Beat.

FREDDIE   You don't have to... you're someone worth waiting for.

DEIRDRE   What?

      FREDDIE fears he has been too vulnerable too soon, and pulls back a little.

FREDDIE   I could stay here. Wait. Isabelle's still asleep, I guess.

DEIRDRE   Yeah. If I ran to the clinic – they all know our family, they'd squish me in. She probably wouldn't even notice.

FREDDIE   Plus, I used to babysit my little sisters.

DEIRDRE   Yeah. Good point. Really?

FREDDIE   Yeah. Janice and Sasha. They're twenty and twenty-two. But not... when I babysat them.

DEIRDRE   Right. Perfect. So, you have experience...

FREDDIE   They're alive today...

DEIRDRE   ...you're trustworthy. Great. I'll be right back.

      They stand up.

DEIRDRE   She's had her meds, Mrs. Harper's phone number is in here. Um. The clinic's right beside Stubbs, and that's only three blocks away, so – but, um. I'll take the car just so... I'll be right back.

FREDDIE   Okay.

      DEIRDRE lunges at FREDDIE, kissing him wholeheartedly and holding on to him for the first time. She pulls away and loses her balance.

DEIRDRE   Geez.

> *She exits, and FREDDIE sits, looking pretty pleased with himself. She returns immediately, to grab her keys and purse. FREDDIE laughs.*

I'm a little distracted. Bye!

FREDDIE   See yuh.

> *The door closes loudly. FREDDIE relaxes back on the couch.*

I'll wait for you. Here.

VIII. I Seen One Before

> *FREDDIE picks up the* Jonathan Livingston Seagull *book. He turns to his favourite part and reads it, smiling. He looks around for a pencil and circles it, writing a comment beside it. He puts it back. He goes to the kitchen and returns with a square from the tray of sweets. Just as he relaxes into the couch again...*

ISABELLE   *(from the bed)* Mom! MOOOOOOOOOM!

> *FREDDIE rushes over to ISABELLE's side.*

FREDDIE   Hey, Isabelle. It's Freddie. Seven Horses. With the vacuum?

ISABELLE   What you doing?

FREDDIE   I'm babysitting you.

ISABELLE   How could you babysit me?

FREDDIE   I just... hang out. What do you mean?

ISABELLE   I haf' go pee.

FREDDIE   Okay.

ISABELLE   I don't pee the bed. I pee in the pot.

FREDDIE   Well... great. It's good... not to... pee... where you sleep.

ISABELLE Are you taking me to the pot?

FREDDIE Sure.

ISABELLE Do you want to hold my hand on the way to the pot?

FREDDIE Sure. Come on. Let's go before we have to do more laundry.

> *FREDDIE helps her out of bed. They walk to the bathroom, hand in hand. FREDDIE returns immediately and sits on the couch. ISABELLE returns to her room, shedding clothing on the way – she is down to her panties and undershirt. She gets back into bed.*

ISABELLE Freddie! I'm goin' to bed now!

FREDDIE Okay, goodnight!

ISABELLE Freddie, I have to be tucked in tight!

FREDDIE Coming.

> *FREDDIE goes to ISABELLE and tucks her in way too tight on purpose – making a game of it. ISABELLE giggles.*

There you go – a bug in a rug. Good? *(pretend threatening)* Do you want it tighter, 'cause I can—

ISABELLE No! No, that's good.

FREDDIE Okay. Anything else?

ISABELLE Kiss goodnight.

FREDDIE Well, now I think you're just stalling. Deirdre thinks you're asleep, you know. I'd be in big trouble if she knew you were awake. Next you're gonna ask me to read you a story – I know all the tricks.

ISABELLE Kiss me, Freddie!

FREDDIE You must be sisters…

> *ISABELLE purses her lips and FREDDIE gives her*
> *a quick peck on the cheek.*

ISABELLE   I could see your penis. I seen one before.

FREDDIE   Okay. Goodnight, then.

> *FREDDIE turns out the light in ISABELLE's room. He*
> *stops leaving when ISABELLE says "Hey!"*

ISABELLE   Hey! Look. I do this sometimes and it feels nice.

> *ISABELLE is rubbing herself under the covers.*
> *FREDDIE exits into the living room.*

FREDDIE   Okay, goodnight, Isabelle. See you later. Sweet
dreams.

> *FREDDIE walks over to the doorway, hoping to see*
> *DEIRDRE returning. He paces back and forth and we*
> *hear ISABELLE moaning. FREDDIE plugs his ears*
> *and starts to sing. ISABELLE joins in "round" style.*

FREDDIE & ISABELLE   Row, row, row your boat...

> *After a few lines of singing, DEIRDRE enters with*
> *a small paper bag from Stubb's pharmacy.*

DEIRDRE   What are you doing?

FREDDIE   Nothing. Nothing, just waiting for you to get back.

DEIRDRE   I thought she was sleeping.

FREDDIE   Yeah, she was, but... she had to go to the washroom.

DEIRDRE   Oh. Good. Thanks for doing that. I couldn't get in to
the doctor, but I picked up some stuff anyway. Since I was
there.

FREDDIE   Cool. I should get going, I guess. It's getting late.

DEIRDRE   Okay. You could stay. We didn't even eat yet.

> *FREDDIE is trying to think of an excuse to leave*
> *because of the embarrassment ISABELLE made him*
> *feel.*

I can put a casserole in. It'll take twenty minutes at most.

FREDDIE   Sure.

ISABELLE   Hi, Dreary!

DEIRDRE   Hello, Isabelle! You should be sleeping! I think there's a lasagna.

FREDDIE   Oh, yeah, I – I love lasagna. Okay. Thanks.

DEIRDRE   You're welcome.

> *DEIRDRE heads toward the kitchen.*

ISABELLE   Freddie! Freeeeeeeeddie!

DEIRDRE   Do you mind tucking her in? *(He hesitates.)* It's okay, she won't bite.

FREDDIE   Okay.

> *DEIRDRE leaves to the kitchen.*

ISABELLE   Freddie!

FREDDIE   I'm coming.

> *FREDDIE stays at ISABELLE's doorway.*

ISABELLE   Freddie, my sheets came out.

FREDDIE   Well, no wonder.

ISABELLE   Freddie, you want to see?

FREDDIE   Isabelle, you shouldn't talk like that to people. It makes them feel embarrassed. And it's not safe. You could get in big trouble.

> *DEIRDRE goes to the living room and sits on the couch.*

ISABELLE   I won't get in trouble. I don't like trouble. I'm good.

FREDDIE   Yes, you are a good girl. So don't talk about this okay? Unless it's with Deirdre, or… a doctor or something. Goodnight.

ISABELLE   I sorry, Freddie. I promise not to talk like that again to you. Am I bad?

FREDDIE   No, Isabelle. I just don't want you to get hurt.

ISABELLE   'Kay.

FREDDIE   Goodnight.

ISABELLE   Goodnight, Freddie.

IX. Baptism by Fire

FREDDIE joins DEIRDRE on the couch.

DEIRDRE   Everything okay?

FREDDIE   Yeah.

DEIRDRE   I've made you uncomfortable, haven't I?

FREDDIE   Ah, nah. Just—Isabelle—I haven't babysat in awhile. I'm out of practice.

DEIRDRE   Does it make you nervous? How she is?

FREDDIE   No! No, not at all. I'm cool.

DEIRDRE   Well, most people—

FREDDIE   Deirdre, seriously. It doesn't bother me at all. I'm fine.

DEIRDRE   I guess I know that you're not – "most people." You… I didn't mean to spit it out like that. About the sex, I mean.

FREDDIE   That's cool. It's good to know I'm not the only one thinking it – I mean, not that I don't think of anything else, but, I am the lesser gender here, I'll admit that. Some guys are really disgusting, and I'm a guy, so I appreciate how frank you were, naturally.

DEIRDRE   It was a little soon, though, huh?

FREDDIE   Well, everything is relative… I suppose compared to …compared to everyone else I've ever dated, yes. It was soon.

DEIRDRE   Do you think I'm slutty now?

FREDDIE   Jesus! No, no I don't. That's a strong word, that.

DEIRDRE   I'm really not slutty. I think I'll enjoy it, but I haven't technically... as I said—I mean, actual... uh... the... I mean, I've had—I like... geez. I'd be interested in...

FREDDIE   Deirdre. You're okay. *(He touches her gently on her knee, to reassure her.)* I'm not going anywhere.

> *They lace their fingers together, exploring that small area of each other.*

DEIRDRE   Have you dated a lot of other girls?

FREDDIE   Okay, again – that's fairly soon for that question. I'd hate for you to ask me that and then think that I'm... slutty.

DEIRDRE   You think men can be sluts?

FREDDIE   Sure. Like I said, growing up with sisters...

DEIRDRE   That's so great. That you think that. That you don't have double standards. My mom would've liked you.

FREDDIE   Oh, yeah? Was your mom pretty open about that kind of thing?

DEIRDRE   No! Heck, no. She's cool, but we're still Catholic.

FREDDIE   Right. But Isabelle... she must know something about that sort of thing? I mean... in Junior High or whatever, someone must have explained what was going on with her body, right?

DEIRDRE   Oh, yeah. My mom used to say that Izzy was more informed than I was. If she knew about what little I've done "out of wedlock" – she'd freak.

FREDDIE   Hm.

DEIRDRE   Anyway, yeah... that's one thing Izzy came across long before I did – the whole sexuality thing. Actually grade six was the first time she was sent home from school for "inappropriate behaviour."

FREDDIE   The *first* time.

DEIRDRE   Yeah. She doesn't... um, how can I... she never seems to connect a punishment to her – whatever it is she shouldn't have done. Or... consequences, I guess. She doesn't have too good a head for them.

FREDDIE   But – wouldn't they know that? The teachers? And your mom, for that matter? That there was no point in "punishing" Isabelle for something that she doesn't think is wrong?

DEIRDRE   Oh, you don't know. She can be so... you wanna – *(makes strangling gesture)* you just forget that she's not the same as us. It's like her brain somehow skips over all of the times she's been scolded for a thing, you know? Like with the... "inappropriate behaviour"? She'll just... ha! She wants it when she wants it, and it doesn't matter if we're in the grocery store, or at the library, at mass – anywhere. Mom was always telling her to "keep her secrets in the bedroom."

FREDDIE   Right. Catholic. *(long struggling beat)* That's... that's too bad. I mean, if they... fuck. Hm. Okay. It would make Isabelle think that sexuality is bad, not the appropriateness of her actions in a certain context.

DEIRDRE   Yeah, but realistically she could never be in an adult relationship. So we sort of have to discourage her from all of it.

FREDDIE   All the more reason she shouldn't be told not to...

DEIRDRE   Nononono. It's too... it's hard enough to explain why she shouldn't touch the stove when it's hot, so you just tell her not to go near it at all. And still she'll put her hand on the burner even when she's already done it a dozen times. With sex, she'd get a lot more than burnt if anything... *(sigh)* complicated explanations are kinda wasted on her.

FREDDIE   Have you tried?

DEIRDRE   Of course. Like I said, she seemed fine until about grade three. She could... learn. She was treated just like anyone else. We just thought she was a little wilder than most of the kids our age. Hyper. You know, keep her off sugar and—

FREDDIE   Was she the only Indian at your school?

DEIRDRE   Um. I don't know.

FREDDIE   Oh, come on Deirdre. You didn't notice?

DEIRDRE   Well, I think she was, but sometimes you can't tell.

FREDDIE   Okay… and what about Isabelle's real family? Do they know who adopted her?

DEIRDRE   How could they? She was given up the day she was born. And nobody's ever tried to find her.

FREDDIE   As far as you know… how did – when they realized Isabelle was… somehow slower. What happened?

DEIRDRE   What do you mean?

FREDDIE   Well, your parents, did they…. *(new approach)* Lots of times Native kids end up getting shuffled around the foster care system. Even if they were adopted once.

DEIRDRE   That's – we wouldn't… Isabelle has been such a blessing. Yes, it's hard sometimes. Really hard. And I'm sure that does happen with a lot of other families, but we have such a faith in—

FREDDIE   No. *(DEIRDRE is puzzled, silenced.)* Okay. Stop right there. I don't wanna hear… the woman who gave birth to her, where was she from? They Blood?

DEIRDRE   Um… my Dad always said her birth mom was Blackfoot.

FREDDIE   Blood is Blackfoot, Deirdre. There's Kainai, Siksika and Pikani – all Blackfoot. "Kainai" is Blood, Blood is Blackfoot.

DEIRDRE   Oh, sorry. They don't teach this sort of thing in school, you know. *(trying to joke about it)* But four months on memorizing the rivers of Alberta – now that's a vital component of every child's education.

FREDDIE   It just doesn't even occur to you.

   Silence.

DEIRDRE   Pardon? I don't know—

FREDDIE   So how Catholic are you?

>   *Beat.*

DEIRDRE   I don't know how to answer that.

FREDDIE   You've never thought about it at all? You just do what your parents tell you? All the time?

DEIRDRE   *(beat)* What did I say? Why are you acting like this?

FREDDIE   I'm just asking you a question.

DEIRDRE   You didn't want me to talk about God, and now you're asking me and I don't know what to say.

FREDDIE   You have choices, Deirdre. You don't have to do what your parents did.

DEIRDRE   I know that. *(FREDDIE waits for an answer.)* What? I know it feels good to pray when I'm sad or really thankful for something. I know I like the stories I hear at mass. I – I like the part where you shake hands with the people around you – "peace be with you." That's it. That's what I think.

>   *FREDDIE stays silent. Long uncomfortable silence.*

So? What? Is that too Catholic for you? I don't understand why it's so important—

FREDDIE   Isabelle's people are not Catholic. Whatever tribe she's from. She's a grown woman and she knows nothing about her own people.

DEIRDRE   We. Are her – no. I. Am her people. That's it. I'm all she has.

FREDDIE   Yeah, because the rest of her people were taken from her the day your parents walked into the hospital and probably paid some nurse—

DEIRDRE   That's not what happened—

FREDDIE   Just bring 'em up white. And we can all pretend they've disappeared.

DEIRDRE   Freddie, I don't want anyone to disappear.

> *He moves to leave.*

FREDDIE   Right.

DEIRDRE   My parents thought they couldn't have children, and so they... we love Isabelle. Very much. We have been running to stand still with her since day one. We would never even think of – what? *Returning* her? Is that what you're saying?

FREDDIE   Oh, I'm sure. I'm sure your family's been an exemplary case of charitable civilized people whose hearts have gone out to the needy. You've been very kind, I'm sure. And those ungrateful people – do they even know what you've done for them?

DEIRDRE   You're not even talking to me.

FREDDIE   Your mother probably... fuck. My mom is terrified to talk to me. I ask about her childhood and she says "what would you want to hear about that for?" She's been so brainwashed by people like you and that she doesn't even feel the desire to know her people anymore – herself. It's been beaten out of her.

DEIRDRE   I'm sorry that... "people like" – what, white people? All white people are brainwashing?—

FREDDIE   And still, every Sunday, off to mass – same as your mom did, I guess! So why does it... Ah, fuck! Who cares? Why do I bother.

> *He hurries toward the door.*

...Just... do your thing to our father who art in heaven if it really makes you feel so much better when you're having a bad day. Peace be with you, Deirdre. I'm outta here.

DEIRDRE   I... I'm... Freddie! I don't know what to say.

> *FREDDIE stops at the door. They are quiet and he lingers. DEIRDRE cannot look his way.*

FREDDIE   She asked me, almost right away. *(silence)* Isabelle. She asked "are you a Indian" – with such... it's just... it makes me mad. Fuckin' pisses me off.

DEIRDRE   I'm sorry. But she's my sister. My real sister. Do you understand?

> *FREDDIE nods.*

There's a lot... that I want for her. That I will give her.

> *Silence.*

FREDDIE   Huh... I don't know why I said that. 'Bout my mom... I didn't mean to say that. That has nothing to do with you. I don't want to – talk to you like that. Why would I say that?

> *DEIRDRE walks toward him.*

I'm so sorry. I didn't mean to do that.

DEIRDRE   Freddie. You can talk to me. Whatever you want.

FREDDIE   I shouldn't have said that. And your mom... you just lost her... unh. I'm so sorry.

> *Beat.*

DEIRDRE   I don't... want you to be mad at me, and I feel like I've done something wrong.

FREDDIE   No—

DEIRDRE   I don't want you to think I'm stupid. And I don't want you to leave.

> *FREDDIE hangs his head. DEIRDRE moves closer to him. She takes FREDDIE's hands. He finally looks in her eyes.*

I'm so sorry.

FREDDIE   I'm sorry. I'm a prick. You don't need to hear – I didn't mean to say it like that. Just because you're Catholic, it doesn't... ugh!

> *She kisses his face and then looks him in the eye.*

DEIRDRE   You don't have to tread lightly with me.

> *DEIRDRE takes FREDDIE's hand and leads him back to sit with her on the couch.*

FREDDIE   The next time I start lecturing, just punch my lights out and I'll apologize when I come to, okay?

DEIRDRE   Okay.

FREDDIE   I'd love to say I won't do it again, but, I just.... The shit my mom went through, you know? I feel like the only way I can take some of it on is to get crazy mad. I'm so fucking angry. And there's no point. It doesn't help anything. I can't... she crosses herself and prays before every meal. I mean... she goes to mass every Sunday morning and sometimes on Saturdays, too. And she knows... I don't... I don't get it! And it makes me nuts.

> *A moment while DEIRDRE summons her courage.*

DEIRDRE   Isabelle... has these moments. She's just sitting there, colouring or watching TV and then she'll look at me and I see this... clarity in her eyes. This big huge presence and I'm sure she's suddenly going to speak to me like she's... normal. Like she's all there. And in a blink, she's herself again – smiling and sweet and... slow. It used to make me so sad. But one day I realized that there is a piece of Isabelle that would make her whole, I can feel it. It's just not here. So where is it? It makes sense to me that God takes care of it. The brilliant part of her. Isabelle makes me believe in God. There must be something that makes your mom believe – something beautiful that she hopes to meet up with when she leaves this world.

FREDDIE   I think I'm gonna have to marry you.

DEIRDRE   You probably say that to every girl who busts your crayons. And anyway, I think you're gross.

> *Long beat as FREDDIE and DEIRDRE stare into one another. They understand one another. They have a consuming, healing kiss and then hold one another.*

X. Camp Out

DEIRDRE   I can't believe you've lived here my whole life and I didn't get to meet you until now.

FREDDIE   Yeah, well, you don't get out much.

> *They laugh and then lose themselves in another long kiss. DEIRDRE restrains herself with some difficulty.*

DEIRDRE   Come by tomorrow.

FREDDIE   Okay.

DEIRDRE   Unless… it's kind of a safe time of the month. And with a prophylactic…

FREDDIE   I don't – I would've thought that was a bit on the presumptuous side. I didn't bring any with me.

> *DEIRDRE grabs the pharmacy bag and holds it up. FREDDIE is speechless.*

DEIRDRE   Of course. *(She breathes deeply and deadpans.)* Well, if we're getting married, maybe we should wait.

> *She lets him worry a moment, and then loses her composure and laughs.*

Oh, you should see yourself! Ah hahaha!

FREDDIE   That's hilarious.

DEIRDRE   I could have fun with that – you actually thought I might be insane for a minute there. Funny.

FREDDIE   Yeh. Very funny. My God, sex, religion, that about covers it.

DEIRDRE   No kidding. Well, it explains why I've never seen you before. You wouldn't have been at Sunday mass at ol' St. Pat's. That's about the extent of my so called social life.

FREDDIE   St. Anne's. *(beat)* We live on the North side.

DEIRDRE   You went to church?

FREDDIE   My mom. I went until I was eighteen. Out of respect for her – misguided though she may be. As soon as I moved out, the obligation ended, as far as I'm concerned.

> *Beat.*

DEIRDRE   Well, you'll be amused to know that you're gonna have me stuck in a confessional for hours for the things I'm thinking about you.

> *FREDDIE gets shy. They have a good deep make-out.*
> *FREDDIE retracts.*

FREDDIE   Okay, we'll have to do something else or I'm going to lose my mind.

DEIRDRE   Right. Well, "M*A*S*H" is on, but not 'til later.

> *Beat. DEIRDRE can't think of anything else.*

DEIRDRE   I've got laundry to fold.

FREDDIE   Woohoo! Dibs on the sock matching!

> *They laugh.*

Can I?— I want to stay the night. We don't have to… I just want to hang out and be in the same room with you. As much as I can.

DEIRDRE   Are you imaginary?

> *She pinches him.*

FREDDIE   Ow! You're supposed to pinch yourself.

> *She laughs.*

DEIRDRE   The sofa bed is clean.

> *They pull out the sofa bed.*

FREDDIE   Well, I'm only staying over if it has one of those really lumpy mattresses so the bar digs into my spinal cord.

DEIRDRE   Well then, you're in for a real treat.

> *He leaps onto the bed and stretches out.*

FREDDIE   Perfect.

DEIRDRE   I'm gonna get some blankets.

FREDDIE   I'll help you...

DEIRDRE   It's all right. Actually, you can check on the lasagna.

FREDDIE   Done.

> *DEIRDRE exits to the basement and FREDDIE heads for the kitchen. ISABELLE sits up in bed. She plucks her pink baby dolls from the carpet. She puts them on over her undies and does some ballerina stretches while standing on the bed. She leaps off the bed. She creeps into the living room, looking about to see if anyone is coming. When she hears FREDDIE coming, she strikes a starting pose.*

It's not even... *(He turns to go tell DEIRDRE that she forgot to turn the oven on, but sees ISABELLE instead.)* Hey. What are you doing up?

> *ISABELLE begins a slow measured ballet for FREDDIE, and he tries not to laugh. DEIRDRE enters with linens and FREDDIE furiously gestures toward ISABELLE, but DEIRDRE has seen this before.*

DEIRDRE   Oh, Miss Isabelle, I wasn't expecting an encore performance so soon. Where did you fly in from so suddenly? Paris? *(ISABELLE shakes her head.)* Moscow? *(head shake)* Somewhere closer, probably...

FREDDIE   Winnipeg?

> *ISABELLE freezes in an ungraceful pose.*

ISABELLE   My room.

DEIRDRE   That's quite the trip.

FREDDIE   She's probably still jet-lagged.

DEIRDRE   You're quite lucky to be a witness to this rare performance, you realize.

FREDDIE   Oh, I do.

DEIRDRE   Isabelle, hon, you have to stay in bed and get plenty of rest until you feel better. You scared everyone a great deal today, and the doctor wants me to bring you in again in a week. If you're still sick, they're gonna take you away from me. Come on, back to bed. You still have cuckoo drugs in your system.

> *DEIRDRE tries to guide ISABELLE back to her room. ISABELLE plants herself and clenches her fists.*

ISABELLE   DON'T! I'M GONNA GET ANGRY!

DEIRDRE   Okay. Calm down. It's okay. What do you want to do, Isabelle? Because I need you to stay warm and rest, but you don't want to go to bed. How can we work this out? Do you have any good ideas? *(ISABELLE nods.)* Okay. Tell me.

> *ISABELLE points at FREDDIE.*

Freddie. *(beat)* What? You want him to leave?

> *ISABELLE shakes her head fiercely and makes whining noises.*

Isabelle. You're not a child. Quit being silly and use your words.

ISABELLE   I want him go bed, too.

DEIRDRE   Do you remember when Mom told you about inappropriate touching of others? That would include this, Isabelle. Freddie cannot go to your bed with you because you and Freddie are not man and wife.

> *FREDDIE chokes on a laugh. DEIRDRE whispers to him fiercely.*

Shut up. *(back to ISABELLE)* Do you remember swimming? Think of the trouble you got in a few weeks ago at swimming – with Devin. Go to your room.

ISABELLE   NO!

FREDDIE   Can I?… sorry. Um, what if we all have a camp out in the living room?

ISABELLE   Another camp out?

FREDDIE Why not? You two can take this luxury sofa bed and I can stay on the floor – do you guys have a sleeping bag?

ISABELLE We have four sleeping bags. One is green and that's my dad's. One is red and that's my mom's. Mine and Dreary's are blue, but mine is the stripes on the inside one.

DEIRDRE It's fine with me if you don't mind sleeping on the carpet.

FREDDIE Nope. Not a bit. Hey, it's clean, right? Sleeping bags in the basement?

DEIRDRE Yeah. *(DEIRDRE throws down a fitted sheet onto the sofa bed.)* Past my bed, to the left, hanging by the washer and dryer there. Watch your step, the basement's not finished.

FREDDIE Right.

DEIRDRE There's an air mattress down there, too. Should be folded up near the Coleman on the shelf.

FREDDIE That's okay. I'd rather sleep on the floor than spend two hours blowing it up.

DEIRDRE Okay. It's your funeral.

ISABELLE The opposite of a birthday.

> *ISABELLE climbs onto the bed.*

DEIRDRE Izzy, I have to put a sheet on there first.

ISABELLE I don't like a sheet.

FREDDIE So... I'll just pop down to the basement. Did you want to come with me?

> *DEIRDRE moves toward him as though by magnetic force and then shrugs and motions to ISABELLE, who is bouncing around, squealing, entangled in the sheet. He smiles and exits SL.*

DEIRDRE Isabelle, you are a pain in the ass. You have no idea how much you owe me.

ISABELLE Ass. Ass. Ass ass ass.

DEIRDRE   Get up. Isabelle! Okay, screw it.

> *DEIRDRE drops the sheets and follows FREDDIE.*

ISABELLE   Screw it. Screw it. Screwbie doobie poo it.

> *The phone rings. ISABELLE screams, startled, then giggles and answers the phone.*

XI. What Happened

ISABELLE   Heddo?

> *Light up on MRS. HARPER in a robe and drinking another Irish Coffee.*

MRS. HARPER   Hey, kiddo. It's Mo.

ISABELLE   Hi, Mrs. Harper Mo.

MRS. HARPER   What are you doing answering the phone? Where's your sister?

ISABELLE   She likes Freddie and he went downstairs for the sleeping bags and so she went downstairs, too. We having a camp out.

MRS. HARPER   All three of yuh?

ISABELLE   Yes. And Freddie babysitted me and I feeled it and he said but don't talk about that.

MRS. HARPER   What did you say, Isabelle?

ISABELLE   Nothing.

MRS. HARPER   Isabelle, you have to tell me. Did you say Freddie babysat you?

> *ISABELLE cannot remember what she was told not to talk about.*

ISABELLE   No. Yes. He babysitted me.

MRS. HARPER   And what happened, Isabelle? He tucked you in?

ISABELLE No. Yes. Really tight. He lifted me and tipped me over and tucked me really tight and I laughed and laughed.

MRS. HARPER And then he turned out the lights and you went to sleep?

ISABELLE No.

MRS. HARPER What happened, Isabelle? Did he tickle you? *(beat)* Did he touch you?

ISABELLE Not s'posed to tell. I scared they – he come… I say I saw a penis before. And that middle hole…

MRS. HARPER Oh, my God. Did he do something to you, Isabelle? Where is Deirdre? Put her on the phone, sweetie.

> *ISABELLE hears DEIRDRE and FREDDIE returning and quickly hangs up. Light out on MRS. HARPER.*

ISABELLE I didn' say nothing.

DEIRDRE About what?

ISABELLE Nothing.

DEIRDRE You're insane.

> *DEIRDRE and FREDDIE arrange the sleeping bags.*

FREDDIE You know, I just thought of something. I don't have a toothbrush.

DEIRDRE We have a little travel one that nobody's ever used. It's under the sink.

ISABELLE Yeah, under the sink.

FREDDIE Great, thanks. And… floss?

DEIRDRE Yeah. Medicine cabinet.

FREDDIE Oo. Is it waxed or unwaxed?

> *DEIRDRE and ISABELLE look at FREDDIE curiously.*

Sorry. My dad's a dentist.

DEIRDRE Doctor Seven Horses? Really?

FREDDIE Doctor Walters. My mom was Seven Horses.

DEIRDRE Wow. Unwaxed.

FREDDIE Beggars can't be choosers, right?

ISABELLE Right.

FREDDIE Okay. I'll go in first, 'cause girls take forever.

> *On DEIRDRE's prompting, ISABELLE throws
> a pillow at FREDDIE.*

Hey!

> *ISABELLE laughs uproariously.*

DEIRDRE Will you be okay tooo… find everything?

FREDDIE Yeah. *(catching her hint)* No! I'm all confused and
I need your help.

DEIRDRE Okay. Be right back, Iz.

> *DEIRDRE and FREDDIE hurry off to make out in the
> bathroom. ISABELLE realizes she's alone and then
> follows them.*

ISABELLE Hey!

DEIRDRE / FREDDIE Isabelle! / Whoa!

ISABELLE What you're doing there?

FREDDIE Holy shit.

> *DEIRDRE drags ISABELLE into the living room by
> the arm.*

DEIRDRE Did you ever think that maybe you should knock on
the door before you just come barging in?

ISABELLE But the door was open.

DEIRDRE Just get in bed and stay there.

ISABELLE You're mean.

DEIRDRE   Never mind!

> *Beat.*

Isabelle, you have to understand something. I like Freddie and he likes me. We're gonna want to be alone sometimes. *(ISABELLE turns away from her.)* Listen, when you're feeling better, you're gonna play at Mrs. Harper's sometimes, okay? Doesn't that sound fun?

ISABELLE   I guess.

DEIRDRE   Oh, come on. Don't you think Mrs. Harper's funny?

ISABELLE   Yes.

DEIRDRE   Well, then? Won't it be fun to spend time at her house?

ISABELLE   I think she's mad at me.

DEIRDRE   Why would she be mad at you?

> *ISABELLE merely shrugs. FREDDIE returns.*

FREDDIE   It's all yours.

DEIRDRE   Did you manage with our low-budget floss?

FREDDIE   Yeh. I think I only lost the one layer of enamel.

DEIRDRE   Isabelle thinks Mrs. Harper is mad at her.

ISABELLE   MO!

DEIRDRE   And apparently she's grouchy again. See if you can fix her before I smother her.

ISABELLE   DON'T SMOTHER! HUG DON'T HIT!

> *DEIRDRE exits to the bathroom, shaking her head. FREDDIE hesitantly sits on the edge of the bed furthest from ISABELLE.*

FREDDIE   What's wrong, Isabelle?

ISABELLE   Shut up.

> *FREDDIE does.*

Why your bed is over there?

FREDDIE   On this side of the bed?

ISABELLE   Yeah.

FREDDIE   Because Deirdre is scared of the dark.

ISABELLE   Really?

FREDDIE   That's the rumour.

ISABELLE   Why your bed can't be in the middo?

FREDDIE   Uh. Well, the bed isn't really big enough for—

> *ISABELLE points firmly to the foot of the bed.*

Oh. At the foot? Okay. I can set up down there. Will you be happier?

ISABELLE   *(angrily)* Yes!

FREDDIE   Don't sound too convincing, but I'll give it a try. Just so you're not mad anymore. *(He moves his sleeping bags.)* Better? Isabelle? Izzy? Are you already sleeping?

> *He walks around to ISABELLE's side of the bed and shakes her feet.*

Isabelle? Wow, you really crashed—

ISABELLE   DON'T YOU EVEN TOUCH ME! GET AWAY!

> *DEIRDRE comes running in with a toothbrush in her hand and sees FREDDIE throw his hands up and step back, with ISABELLE uncovered from having sat up abruptly.*

DEIRDRE   What's going on?

ISABELLE   *(crying)* I'm bad.

FREDDIE   She asked me to move my bed down there, so I did, then I was checking if she was sleeping and she just…

DEIRDRE   I'll be right back.

ISABELLE lies down, sulking. FREDDIE walks to the safe side of the bed. DEIRDRE exits and returns wearing short sleeveless pajamas and carrying a bottle of lotion. She sits on the bed, legs crossed beneath her, and puts lotion on her arms. FREDDIE is distracted by the sensuality of this action.

Hey, I was thinkin' about... how come your friends are mad at you for going away to Toronto? You'd think they'd be kind of impressed. Um – I am.

FREDDIE   D'you ever hear the term "apple"?

DEIRDRE   Like, the Big Apple?

FREDDIE   You are so beautiful.

DEIRDRE blushes and starts putting lotion on her legs. FREDDIE is mesmerized by this.

DEIRDRE   I would love to go to New York sometime. Toronto, too. Oh, and Paris. I know a lot of people think the French are rude, but those are usually people who can't be bothered to learn a foreign language.

DEIRDRE is finishing up with the lotion, and FREDDIE is too tortured to watch anymore so he climbs into his sleeping bag, shifting constantly. He ejects his pants.

You must be tired. Sorry. I'll hurry. I usually do this in the bathroom but I was worried someone would make fun of me for being in there too long.

FREDDIE   It's okay.

DEIRDRE looks at the sleeping ISABELLE.

DEIRDRE   Wow, she's like a rock, poor thing, the meds at the hospital always do this to her. When's the last time you had a sleepover with a girl and her sister?

FREDDIE   Never.

DEIRDRE   Pretty bizarre, huh? Fun, though. Not many guys would bother.

FREDDIE   Well, I'm actually just casing the joint.

> *They both laugh. DEIRDRE kneels down at the end of the bed, overlooking FREDDIE. He reaches up and pulls her down onto the floor. DEIRDRE muffles her own scream.*

Shhh! People are trying to sleep.

DEIRDRE   You brat! You're telling me—

> *FREDDIE moves on top of DEIRDRE, stopping her speech with his mouth. ISABELLE stirs above them.*

ISABELLE   Dreary? Dreary?

> *DEIRDRE and FREDDIE freeze. DEIRDRE silently crawls back onto the bed.*

DEIRDRE   I'm right here, Izzy. *(She soothes her and then leans back over FREDDIE.)* You!

FREDDIE   Oh, yeah, you really put up a fight.

DEIRDRE   This is crazy, I've barely met you and I have no idea who you are, but it just seems right. You staying over, all of the… it's just… somehow okay.

FREDDIE   Okay?

DEIRDRE   No, no… it's amazing.

> *They move to kiss again, and DEIRDRE restrains herself.*

We should sleep.

FREDDIE   Right.

> *DEIRDRE turns off the lamp.*

Sleep. No problem. Cool.

> *FREDDIE shifts around and can't even close his eyes. After a short while, he peeks over the bed to see if DEIRDRE is anticipating a move. She isn't. He lies back down, trying to forget his tortured state. He sits up again, and this time DEIRDRE slowly sits up.*

DEIRDRE   For God's sake. I forgot the lasagna.

FREDDIE   I – I'm sure it'll be okay. You didn't even turn the oven on. It was frozen solid.

DEIRDRE   Whups. Are you sure *you'll* be okay? We haven't eaten since the hospital. You're not hungry?

FREDDIE   For food? No. I'm okay for that.

DEIRDRE   I'm so sorry. Geez, her and her tantrums. Okay, I'll be quiet. Goodnight.

FREDDIE   Okay. Goodnight.

> *DEIRDRE lies back down, so FREDDIE does, too. ISABELLE sighs as she stretches out, getting comfortable. Finally, FREDDIE sits up. He slowly crawls out of his sleeping bag, grabbing his pillow to hide his erection. He steps quietly past the bed.*

I think I'll just… run to the washroom before I go to sleep.

DEIRDRE   You were just there.

FREDDIE   Yeah. Well, I'm gonna have to run there quickly before I have any chance of sleeping at this point.

DEIRDRE   Okay.

FREDDIE   Do you want to come?

DEIRDRE   *(giggling knowingly)* No, thank you. We better wait until I can get to the doctor.

FREDDIE   Right. You're absolutely right.

> *FREDDIE spies the lotion on the side table, zips back to grab it and then exits into the bathroom. After a moment, the doorbell rings.*

DEIRDRE   Freddie? What are you…

> *ISABELLE stirs somewhat. DEIRDRE puts a comforting hand on ISABELLE, then walks over to the front door.*

Who is it?

MRS. HARPER *(offstage)* Deirdre, honey, it's Mrs. Harper. Open the door.

DEIRDRE Mrs. – Mrs. Harper, what are you doing here?

> *MRS. HARPER makes a beeline for ISABELLE. The following scene must be frenetic and fast, with lines overlapping and cutting each other off.*

MRS. HARPER Where is he? Is he still here?

DEIRDRE Freddie? He's in the washroom. Why—

MRS. HARPER Get her jacket and grab your keys. I ran here as fast as I could. Ken has the car up in Grand Prairie. Wake up, Isabelle, come on.

ISABELLE Where we're going?

MRS. HARPER Come on, come with me. We're going to go to my house.

DEIRDRE Mrs. Harper, what is going on here?

MRS. HARPER That boy you brought into your home—

DEIRDRE Freddie? You just met him at the hospital, you said he was a darling.

MRS. HARPER Come on, sweetie. Come on. Why would you leave her in the care of a strange man you met selling vacuum cleaners door to door?

DEIRDRE Mrs. Harper—

ISABELLE I was sleepin'…

MRS. HARPER Do you know what he did? Did you even ask her?

DEIRDRE I don't know what you're talking about. I don't know why you're even here!

> *FREDDIE enters and quickly finds his pants.*

FREDDIE What's going on?

MRS. HARPER You shut your mouth, you know goddamn well what's going on here.

DEIRDRE   Wait a minute here. Don't talk to him like he's some sort of—

ISABELLE   Why I'm in trouble? I dinnit tell nothing, Freddie!

FREDDIE   What?

MRS. HARPER   Do you see? Do you see what he's done to this little girl? You get the hell out of here and away from these girls. Do you have any idea what they've been through?

FREDDIE   Okay, hold on. I don't think anyone has the full story here.

ISABELLE   I sorry, Freddie! I so sorry!

FREDDIE   Isabelle, it's okay.

MRS. HARPER   Don't you talk to her.

DEIRDRE   What's wrong, Isabelle?

MRS. HARPER   It's a bit late for that, Deirdre. Why don't you ask Freddie what happened while you were out?

FREDDIE   Hold on here. You're misunderstanding this. Just let her talk – she'll tell you…

ISABELLE   I dinnit mean to be bad! Ahhhh… *(ISABELLE, past words, is bawling hard.)*

DEIRDRE   I don't understand…

MRS. HARPER   I spoke with Isabelle on the phone while you two were fooling around in the basement. She told me that Freddie was in her room and made her – he had her… oh, dear Jesus, how could you let this happen to this sweet girl?

FREDDIE   That did not happen. Nothing happened. I tucked her in—

ISABELLE   Don't you say! Freddie said not to ever talk about that. He said I would get in—get in—get in trouble… *(She cries again.)*

DEIRDRE   She was shrieking at you—when I was brushing my teeth—like you…

FREDDIE   No.

DEIRDRE   You were standing over her and she was so – so afraid.

FREDDIE   No. Deirdre, no. This is all fucked up. Nothing happened. I tucked her in and she started asking me to – to do things.

MRS. HARPER   How dare you blame this girl? How dare you stand there—

DEIRDRE   You should go.

FREDDIE   Deirdre—

DEIRDRE   Go! Until I can figure out what the hell is going on here.

FREDDIE   Isabelle, tell your sister what happened.

> *He moves toward ISABELLE and MRS. HARPER prevents him.*

DEIRDRE   Please don't talk to her.

FREDDIE   I don't... I can't...

MRS. HARPER   Leave this house.

FREDDIE   I just—

DEIRDRE   Get out!

ISABELLE   I sorry, Freddie. I dinnit mean to tell.

> *FREDDIE grabs his shoes and exits. MRS. HARPER shouts after him.*

MRS. HARPER   Don't you come near these girls again!

> *DEIRDRE walks slowly toward the sofa bed and sits on it.*

Are you okay, Isabelle? Are you hurting at all? Are you sore? This girl should go to a clinic, Deirdre.

ISABELLE   No.

DEIRDRE   The whole reason he was here...

MRS. HARPER   Do you want to stay at my house tonight, honey?

ISABELLE   No, I wanna stay with Deirdre.

MRS. HARPER   Oh, she'll come, too. Deirdre? You'll stay at my house tonight. He could come back here. Come on, Isabelle. We'll get you to bed and you'll feel all better in the morning.

MRS. HARPER and ISABELLE exit.

XII. Epilogue – Separate

DEIRDRE walks over to ISABELLE's bedroom and starts to fill a cardboard box with ISABELLE's things.

DEIRDRE   And she did for awhile. Feel better. We found our space together in this house. Just the two of us. Then she started to feel tired all the time and sick in the mornings. The doctor said she was due in April. For a little while I try to believe that I can look after Isabelle and the baby. But I keep thinking how much it was just to look after Izzy... She gets to take some of her things with her. The Michener Centre has strict policies that are meant to keep other residents from feeling unfavoured. The other things go to the Salvation Army.

ISABELLE enters, in a near catatonic state, wearing a blue robe. DEIRDRE does not acknowledge her.

Her room is small. She shares it with a girl who is barely there. Skin and bones and not a word. Isabelle's not there a month and I move up to Red Deer – even though they don't let family visit for the first year. So I get hired with the cleaning staff at the Michener Centre – graveyard shift. Nobody knows she's my sister. I visit her while she sleeps. Tell her about the things that have happened – real and made-up. Bedtime stories. One story every night. I tell her where her things went. Her favourite things they wouldn't let her keep—the white dresser, her baby dolls, her Barbie car—and I try to think of a good place where they've ended up. I tell her about the night her son was born – pulled from her belly while she slept. I don't tell her how I nearly screamed out loud when I saw his red curly hair, how I had to stop myself from running to find a phone. Call information for Seven Horses. The next night I come in for my shift and the baby is gone – adopted by a rich couple in Indiana.

> ISABELLE sits beside DEIRDRE, not seeing her. DEIRDRE now speaks to ISABELLE. During the following, ISABELLE's blue robe falls open revealing a white hospital gown soaked through with breast milk.

One night while I'm visiting, a nurse comes in, so I pretend to empty the empty garbage can. She doesn't even look my way as she sits you up and pulls down your covers. You're still the same – you don't wake up even if you're seated upright and spoken to. The nurse doesn't ask me to leave. She lifts your nightgown to check your stitches – an angry bright red half moon on your poor belly. I sweep the floor. The nurse reaches for the garbage can, so I hold it up. I see the… cotton gauze, soaked through with milk. The nurse tucks fresh pads inside your gown, to absorb the milk your breasts will not stop making. Milk for a son you will never hold. She finally leaves and I tuck you in. Tight.

> ISABELLE's arms are gently outstretched and upturned, her robe open revealing her unused breast milk seeping through the bright white hospital gown. She is the vision of a ruined woman child in a Virgin Mary blue overdress, her own humanity betraying her, celebrating her.
>
> Blackout.
>
> THE END

• Tara Beagan •

Of Ntlaka'pamux (Thompson River Salish) and Irish Canadian heritage, Tara was born and raised in Alberta. She has found an artistic home in Toronto. Beagan wrote her first play, *Thy Neighbour's Wife* (UnSpun Theatre) in 2004 as a means of enabling her to stretch her acting muscles. The play went on to win the 2005 Dora Mavor Moore Award (Outstanding New Play, Independent) with Beagan receiving an acting nomination for her role in the production. In addition to *Dreary and Izzy*, which premiered through Native Earth Performing Arts at the Factory Studio Theatre, her works to date include: *TransCanada* (also for NEPA) at Harbourfront Centre; *Here, boy!* for halfbreed productions and the 28th annual Rhubarb! Festival at Buddies in Bad Times Theatre; *Mom's Birthday* for Nightwood Theatre's Groundswell Festival; *Bad As I Am* for the 2006 Tarragon Playwright's Unit; "133 Skyway," a short film for Big Soul Productions; and *Home Time* for CBC Radio One. Tara also embraces the delicious madness of working on collective creations such as: *Ever Sick* (Tonto's Nephews and NEPA), *Head-Smashed-In Buffalo Jump* (UnSpun), *Suck and Blow* (Absit Omen), and the ambitious, multi-disciplinary site-specific *Fort York* with Crate Productions.